Store Windows

No.16

Store Windows

No. 16

Martin M. Pegler

VISUAL REFERENCE PUBLICATIONS, INC., New York, NY

Visual Reference Publications, Inc.
302 Fifth Avenue
New York, NY 10001

Distributors to the trade in the United States and Canada
Watson-Guptill
770 Broadway
New York, NY 10003

Distributors outside the United States and Canada
HarperCollins International
10 E. 53rd Street
New York, NY 10022

Library of Congress Cataloging in Publication Data:
Store Windows No. 16

Printed in China
ISBN: 1-58471-124-7
978-1-58471-124-7

Book Design: Judy Shepard

TABLE OF CONTENTS

SPRING

SUMMER/CRUISE & RESORT

FALL

WINTER/CHRISTMAS

INTRODUCTION

For years the American theater has been called "The Fabulous Invalid." Critics have buried it: put the black wreath on the theater door and wrapped their arms in black ribbons. And, every year the theater gasps—moves—shows signs of life and once again refuses to give up the spirit—or the opportunity to breath entertainment life on the stage.

Window displays could also be called "The Fabulous Invalid." They—whoever "they" are —changed the name from "display" to "visual merchandising" and now to "visual presentation." "They" turned the theatrical, stage-like display windows into flat, almost non-dimensional open back windows where the upfront presentation often has to yield to what is going on in the store beyond. We have gone from propping to no props at all and then to giant graphics along with dress forms—and that became the epitome of window dressing during the 1990s and into the 21st century. "They" killed—or at least attempted to murder—display/visual merchandising with budget cuts, staff-cuts, and then by completely obliterating windows all together. The minimal/no-display agenda that swept across the retail scene was the result of economy moves by department store chains and the national chains who then assumed the leading roles in window displays. And yet today, there are not only signs of life—there are signs of a healthy renaissance—a rebirth—a renewed interest in window presentation as street entertainment and an important part of brand identification. It is eye-candy—the lure or the allure of shopping.

The signs of "spring" and rejuvenation that you are seeing in malls, in centers and on shopping streets are now being led by the same national chains that were among the first to give up on props and decoratives. Some of the major department store chains never totally gave up on window display, but "economy" meant simplification—re-use—adapting and restraining talent and imagination of staff—and "all for the sake of economy." Just as retail and fashion exists for change, it takes display/visual presentation to not only affect that change, but to make the change evident to the shoppers on the street. Changing a large graphic is no longer enough! We are beginning to see more lifestyle settings. Sometimes the lifestyle is suggested by a chair, a table, a drape and a plant—or it may be visualized for the shopper in a full room-like setting complete with accessories. While smaller specialty stores are freer to express themselves with humor, attitude and wild imagination, the larger chains must be creative and imaginative and create adaptable displays; displays that will not only adapt to different size and shaped windows, but windows in different spaces and in different parts of the country with different demographics. However, they are doing it and some of these results have been included in this edition of Store Windows.

With each edition of this book we attempt to not only find the newest and most exciting window presentations, we also bring together—from all over the world—the talents that create them. And once again—only for the convenience of showing the displays—we have chaptered them by the four seasons: spring, summer, fall and winter. We hope you look at these images as "ideas"—as "concepts"—as starting points for your own flights of fancy. And—just because we put "Mirror," "Frames," or "Dangles" in our Fall section—doesn't mean that you can't come up with fun ideas that will work at any other time of the year. We have also included promotions where the idea or theme is carried through a series of windows; adapted or altered or accessorized to suit the variety of product offering.

So, put away the wreaths and the dismal black ribbons. Put away the hankies; no tears today! Smile and brighten up. The "patient" is not only recovering and moving up and out on its own but is spreading its good health to other retailers who have been holding back. They too are realizing that display/visual presentation helps to differentiate one store from another—reinforces the store's brand image and adds a smile on the face of the harried shopper. It also puts color into what can be a cold, gray world.

Enjoy!! Display is alive and thriving!

Martin M. Pegler

Store Windows

No. 16

PAPER SPRING @ MARSHALL FIELD'S

MARSHALL FIELD'S, State St., Chicago, IL
DIRECTOR OF WINDOWS: **Amy Meadows**

Gone—but not forgotten!! Marshall Field's may now be a name only cherished in the hearts of old time Chicagoans, but to many of us in the display field, the name and the numerous illustrious display people who create such memorable windows and interior trim, the name Marshall Field's will live on forever. So, as a farewell to a Grand Old Store and a salute to the season of revival, we salute MF by presenting that store's last spring spectacular.

Lovely spring fashions were presented in the cool aqua/white settings filled with floating, flying and fabulous cut-out paper flowers, flower forms and see-through umbrellas. Even the umbrellas were covered with the flower-stenciled motif that introduced these display settings by appearing, in contrast, on the front glass. The viewer on State St. was invited to look past the swirling baroque drawing of flowers, boughs and birds to behold the beige and white fashions worn by white abstract mannequins. The vignettes looked like frozen moments out of an Alvin Alley dance.

We will miss you Marshall Field's and your wonderfully creative displays.

MARSHALL FIELD'S, State St., Chicago, IL
DIRECTOR OF WINDOWS: **Amy Meadows**

SCHREIBMEISTER, Munich, Germany
DESIGN & INSTALLATION: **Gert Mueller**

Once again we return to Munich to salute Gert Mueller and his ability to find new and different ways to make pens, pads, portfolios and sundry stationery items seem romantic and vital throughout a whole season. Using a mixture of natural and artificial materials—from birch branches and birch tree stumps, and entwining vines and twigs to man-made tulips, roses, various flower heads and dozen of faux birds, Gert Mueller creates new and arresting settings in the open back window at Schreibmeister, a Munich stationery institution. Geometric shaped panels, floral prints, pinks and pale violets all add to the Springtime salute rendered in this window.

Etalage B Display also brought the fantasy of Springtime into the Place Alexis-Nihon mall in Montreal. Here they created an enchanted forest by introducing imaginative, larger-than-life birds, flowers and animals that could only exist in a magical environment. Under the creative directorship of Constant Bibeau, Sylvie Champagne and the staff turned the multi-story modern mall into a place of magic and dreams with color and flower filled spaces. That same free-flowing imagination was carried out in the display windows such as are shown here: "Butterflight" as designed by Eric Fleury.

PLACE ALEXIS-NIHON, Montreal, QC
Etalage B Display, Montreal, QC
CREATIVE DIRECTOR: **Constant Bibeau**
DESIGNERS: **Sylvie Champagne, Eric Fleury**

Etalage B Display, a custom display design and installation firm in Montreal working under creative director Constant Bibeau, think daisies—giant overscaled daisies—are the way to greet spring. In the Place Dupuis, an upscale mall, the designer Catherine Begin uses daisy heads and bright yellow panels to introduce an assortment of the mall's retailers to the shoppers on the street. Among the products shown are men's and women's intimate apparel, photography equipment, stationery, baked goods and floral supplies.

PLACE DUPUIS, Montreal, QC
DESIGN FIRM: **Etalage B Display,** Montreal, QC
CREATIVE DIRECTOR: **Constant Bibeau**
DESIGNER: **Catherine Begin**

Je t'aime

Je t'aime

Je t'aime

COACH, Madison Ave., New York, NY

GUCCI, Fifth Ave., New York, NY

The three B's of Springtime: Birds, Butterflies and Bees. Birds fly back from wherever they have gone to—butterflies come out of their colorless cocoons in all their technicolor splendor and wherever there are flowers—the bees are sure to be buzzing about. So—comes spring fashions—the B's are sure to follow.

Butterflies are fluttering amid Coach's display of colorful shoes while a pair of mannequins is all set to snare some butterflies of their own. The well lit abstracts in the open back window are strong enough to draw the viewer closer to see what has been spread out on the grass covered floor.

Butterfly images are attached to blocks of wood to create a unique setting for Gucci's unusual, one-of-a-kind embroidered shirts for men. The "masculine" hunks of rough wood complement the delicacy of the butterfly tracery to add a bit of the macho to the elegant setting.

Butterflies flutter amid the framed floral prints that are lined up on the back wall of Bloomingdale's window. Some of the butterflies have become attached to the sun tanned abstracts up front. Also at Bloomingdale's are the fanciful white wire birdcages that hang and stand in this window. Some blackbirds are in the cages while others fly free and they pick up the black artwork that appears on the front glass and sets the scene for the Rebecca Taylor outfits.

BLOOMINGDALE'S, Lexington Ave., New York, NY

The bee hive is graphically represented by the hexagonal shapes scattered throughout the yellow glow of the Hermes window. Overscaled yellow and black bees carry the Hermes ties and handkerchiefs for the viewer's perusal while other ties and men's fashions are carefully coiled inside the hexagonal boxes made of corrugated board. A mirrored "tree" makes a strong vertical statement in the design.

HERMÈS, E. 57th St., New York, NY

Whether the greenery is grass or growing sprouts or clipped and crisped shrubs and bushes, springtime is green-up time and everything is coming up in assorted shades of green for spring. It is the color of rebirth—of rejuvenation—and of winter's snow being a thing of the past.

Green was the color and the theme for spring at H&M—with topiary-like shrubs filling in the foreground and the green back wall embellished, embroidered and enhanced with ivy like vines creeping and crawling all over the very tall window. Taking advantage of the window's height, the suspended swings in the window are also entwined with ivy and they raise up some of the mannequins off the washed-with-green floor of the window.

Burberry used topiary in a clever and imaginative way. By scooping out openings in their clipped green shrubs, they created effective shadow boxes within which to show case some of their featured leather fashion accessories. Though these were originally shown as Christmas windows, if you take away the snow, take off the doggie blankets and the coats and bring in an aqua sky and some yellow "sunlight" this could be a wonderful spring setting. Some flowers and a few flowering branches overhead wouldn't hurt.

H&M, 34th St., New York, NY

BURBERRY, E. 57th St., New York, NY

ANN TAYLOR, New York, NY

HENRI BENDEL, Fifth Ave., New York, NY

Henri Bendel's display designers clipped a "keyhole" in their shrubbery to afford the viewing public on the street a private look at some intimate apparel. It's one way of looking at it and getting to see what's on the other side of the green wall.

Crisply clipped, grass-covered panels created an outdoors spring-like setting for Ann Taylor's black and white garments. The green color not only sparked the neutral outfits but complemented the gray and green dots that were suspended in other windows as part of this promotion. See "Dots Nice @ Ann Taylor."

BROOKS BROTHERS, Fifth Ave., New York, NY

Popping up in patches amid blankets of snow is grass—a harbinger of spring. The fresh, clear color of green stepping out of the white—or brown earth—tells us that spring is on its way. Whether the grass covers the ground or appears in spots—the message is delivered. Topiary is even greener and more spring-like.

Brooks Brothers is making a big statement in their windows as they cover the floors with green grass mats and back them up with an unending spread of topiary-like foliage across the back wall. The topiary trees, the white Adirondack chairs and croquet set prop out the outdoors scene.

BURBERRY, E. 57th St., New York, NY

COLE HAAN, Fifth Ave., New York, NY

The topiary background across Cole Haan's window provides a spring setting for the terra cotta pots that support the new season's fashion accessories.

Patches of green broken up by a white gravel path bring the large photo blow-up background imagery into dimension and adds texture as well. Burberry's outfits are presented on old fashioned dress forms with wire baskets and cast iron bases.

A little grass goes a long way at T. Eaton where the green grass islands on the selling floor set the theme for the new casual outfits. Grass matting has also been applied around the photo to enhance the out of doors theme.

T. EATON, Toronto, ON, Canada
PHOTOGRAPHER: **Guntar Kravis**

HENRI BENDEL, Fifth Ave., New York, NY

You may not be able to smell them or touch them, but you can see them and see the bright fresh colors that forecast spring fashions. Fabric, plastic or paper—real or synthetic—in pots, urns, vases, pinned onto walls, dripping from ceilings or sprouting up from the floors—life sized or over exaggerated—flowers say spring.

Spring is literally "bustin' out all over" in Henri Bendel's window with a full explosion of oversized paper flower heads in a rainbow of colors. They help the store celebrate "We love spring—We love color" promotion. It may be a little like looking to find "Waldo" but there are polychrome fashion accessories on display in that floral eruption.

Fantasy flowers take over in the Fortunoff window where—here too—oversized flowers take over to set the scene for the unique gifts being presented.

FORTUNOFF, Fifth Ave., New York, NY

VALENTINO, Las Vegas, NV

BROOKS BROTHERS, Fifth Ave., New York, NY

Elegant and refined, Brooks Brothers' high window easily accommodates the tall flowering branches in the very tall urn. The vertical lines are emphasized in this composition. The clothes and background panel carry through the pastel pink and mauve color story accented with black.

A swing seat that serves as a platform or elevation for Valentino's rich fashion accessories is suspended by ropes entwined with silk roses, leavers and ribbons. The subtle pink tones of the background graphic and the scattered petals on the floor complete the setting.

It is all fantasy at Artistic Frame where a mannequin dressed in flowers, petals and foliage is used to introduce the season. Grass matting is laid out on the floor and also twisted into a "wig" for the figure.

ARTISTIC FRAMES,
New York, NY

SAKS FIFTH AVENUE, New York, NY

Just as flower-splattered prints are sure to appear each spring to enliven the fashion scene; you can count on floral graphics to show up as backgrounds for some of the windows that display those fashions.

Black line drawings of giant flower heads, in Saks Fifth Avenues' window, are reproduced on a series of panels that serve as a background for the suntanned semi-abstract mannequins in floral prints and appliqués. The pinks and red are picked up on the background panels to enhance the colors in the garments.

The selection of print and solid separates in Pardueles window get a real boost from the large floral graphic set atop an easel and used to balance the asymmetric composition. Fashion accessories are displayed on and under the central riser.

PARDUELES, Mexico City, Mexico

St. John's simple, Mondrian-inspired screen is filled with black and white floral renderings some of which are highlighted with an ocher/gold color. The black and white outfit has a black and white print and is shown on a realistic mannequin. A central plinth carries a black bag.

NY Look took a look at its spring collection and came up with these big, very big, decorative flower panels to set the scene. Bright, bold and eye-catching.

ST. JOHN, Fifth Ave., New York, NY

NY LOOK, Fifth Ave., New York, NY

SAKS FIFTH AVENUE, New York, NY

"Let a smile be your umbrella"—or "Let it rain, let it rain, let it rain"—"April showers bring May flowers"—or whatever. Whatever it is, an umbrella is a great cover-up—a great prop—and can be used most any time but it works especially well for spring.

Saks filled the back wall of their all-white window with dozens of ordinary black umbrellas in various stages of being opened or closed. In a way it was a giant magnified look at the "umbrella" pattern that was teamed up with black and white separates on the white abstract mannequins in the window. What a fun and attractive way to get the print message across.

At Bendel's they are prepared for all sorts of weather in all sorts of places with the assortment of bags and umbrellas that filled the window. The umbrellas float and fly between the bags and the airplane models in this color filled, light filled display. Travel can be fun but it pays to be prepared for a change in the weather.

Umbrellas are also iconic for fashion photography. The familiar white umbrella is used as a light reflector/deflector and is as much a part of the fashion shoot as the camera, the photographer and the model. Saks Fifth sets up a fashion shoot with a few metal uprights, some theatrical lights and the umbrella to make the light just right for the featured garment. The word-tattooed cut-out silhouette figure provides the final touch. This is a display where the props are all around you just waiting to be assembled and placed.

Tiffany & Co. wants sparkle—lots of sparkle—on its diamond necklace. To provide the right touch of shimmer and shine there is the mosaic mirrored disco ball and the photographer's white umbrella to make sure that the light goes where it is supposed to go. Lots of sparkle and shimmer.

In another Tiffany window a white umbrella sets the scene by announcing the reception is in the garden and the lovely featured china repeats the garden theme. The light plays on the umbrella and the curlicue shadows on the rear wall emphasize the script on the umbrella.

HENRI BENDEL, Fifth Ave., NY

TIFFANY & CO., Fifth Ave., NY

HARVEY NICHOLS: BLOWN AWAY

HARVEY NICHOLS, London, UK
VISUAL MERCHANDISING CONTROLLER: **Janet Wardley**
WINDOW DISPLAY MANAGER: **Laura O'Connor**
PROPS: **Icon Studio** and **Artefacts**
PHOTOGRAPHY: **Michael Taylor**

A bold sweep that adds a new thrill to career dressing. An unfelt but very visible tornado blows through these windows picking up and tossing about reams and reams of curled and furled paper. The "paper trail" floats up and down—in one window and out through another—where once again the HN display team finds new uses for old clichés like filing cabinets, step ladders and old computers. Whether it is targeted at back-to-college or back-to-the-workplace the fashions are boldly presented in a flurry of tossed and swirled paper.

LORD & TAYLOR, Fifth Ave., New York, NY
DIV, VP VISUAL MERCHANDISING & FASHIONS: **Manoel Renha**

What dad is all about is really what golf is all about. So—if dad doesn't think chasing a little ball around miles of grassland—it's OK, he can still wear the smart and stylish casual wear that is on display in L & T's windows.

Green grass mats cover the floors of the windows and in some cases miniature sand traps are indicated. Giant photomurals of golf courses and wonderful sea/sky images create the desired out-of-doors effect and create the settings where these outfits score big. Flags indicate holes, golf balls, golf clubs, golf bags and golf buggies are all used as props. In some of the windows—for a change of pace—the graphics are of golfers on the greens.

To set the theme and carry through on the Dad swing, a green silhouette of a golfer marks the front glass of each window along with the "All About Dad" logo. Additional white lettered words provide more impact—and greater "golf appeal"; Swing, Tempo, Grip, Stance and Alignment.

LORD & TAYLOR, Fifth Ave., New York, NY
DIV, VP VISUAL MERCHANDISING & FASHIONS: **Manoel Renha**

Another time—another look—and another approach to what could be an effective Father's Day promotion. "The Fast Track" introduced Lord & Taylor's new contemporary sportswear collection and it tied in with a showing of motorcycles provided by Fast by Ferracci—a Philadelphia company founded by the Italian national champion motorcycle rider Eraldo Ferracci.

The new collection of clothes included labels such as Fila, Ducati, Retrospettiva, Moonlight Graham and jeans by Mavi, FRX, Hudson and Cabral. The rough and rugged realistic mannequins were backed up with urban-ized settings that included brick walls smothered with motorbiking graphics, cyclone fencing and images of open spaces as well as giant graphics—sliced into three vertical panels—and spread out across some of the back walls. In each display set up there was a slick, shiny and speedy Fast by Ferracci motorcycle and it always appeared up front and center.

Shoppers were invited to visit The Men's Shop, in the store, and register to win a Duicati M620 bike valued at $6595 that was on display on the floor. No purchase necessary. Wouldn't Dad have loved to get that as a Father's Day gift?

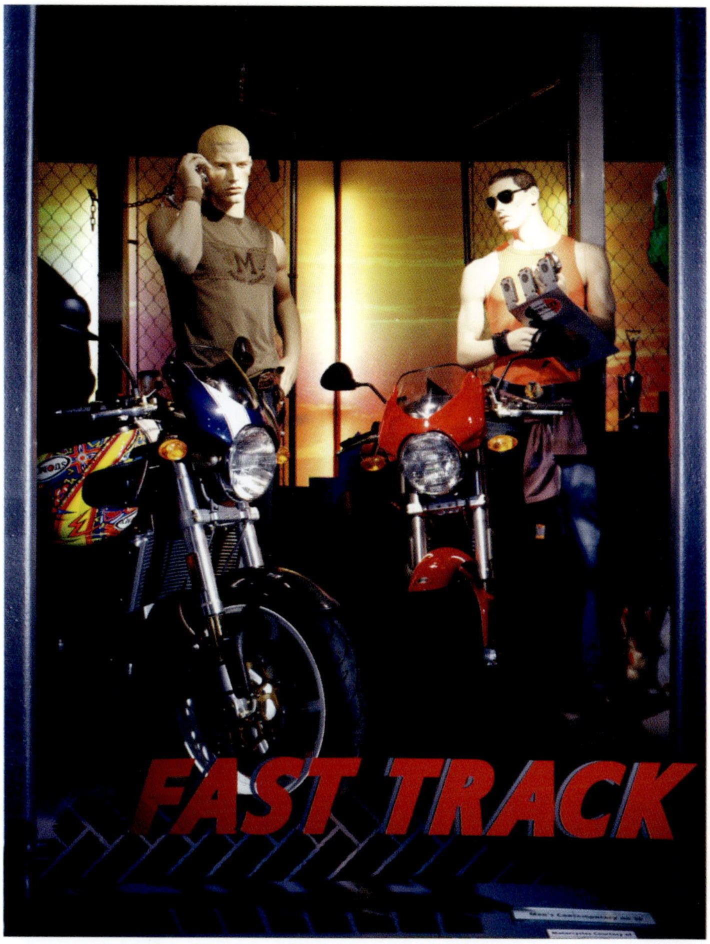

LORD & TAYLOR, Fifth Ave., New York, NY
DIV, VP VISUAL MERCHANDISING & FASHIONS: **Manoel Renha**

BARNEYS NEW YORK, Madison Ave., New York, NY

Good display props don't need to cost lots of money. You really have to look around—and find them. What may be someone else's trash could be a display person's treasure. You don't necessarily have to check out garbage cans but lots of "worthwhile" display props are objects that are tossed away or sitting on the curb just waiting for someone with an "eye" for display value to discover and use them.

From the Barneys images shown here one would think the display department has a full time "trash" collector on staff. In one display it is a collection of electronic "guts" being arranged as artwork while leaky shower heads, faulty plumbing, busted tin buckets and washed up old mops create the display setting enhanced by the strung macaroni "water."

BARNEYS NEW YORK, Madison Ave., New York, NY

BLOOMINGDALE'S, Lexington Ave., New York, NY

SAKS FIFTH AVENUE, New York, NY

Saks Fifth Avenue created a hanging sculpture out of beat-up, wrecked supermarket wagons loaded with several day's worth of junk pick up. Bergdorf complements their overscaled saw and hammer with a multitude of rusty, ruined old tools, hardware and nails right out of some worn down handyman's shop.

Next time it may be "the kitchen sink"! However, for this COOL COOL promotion, the useless old fridge has been revived and given a new coat of paint and a new meaning in Bloomingdale's promotion for ponchos. It may not make ice cubes but it certainly sends out enough snow to bury the floor.

BERGDORF GOODMAN, Fifth Ave., New York, NY

CALVIN KLEIN, (above and below), New York, NY

Household items bring interest —intrigue and sometimes a sense of fun to a window display. Some of these "props" are just sitting and waiting to be discovered or recovered and given a new meaning in a display set-up. Sometimes, as illustrated here, that "prop" is outside—discarded—ignored—just waiting to be carted away with the trash. When re-discovered these worn, tired, battered and bruised items can either be left "as is" or given a new look with a coat of paint and given a second chance as they add something special to a fashion presentation.

Who would ever think that there was still life in the old doors that add a new "slant" to the Calvin Klein fashions in CK's Fifth Avenue windows? The reclining, resting headless forms look perfect a-tilt against the bruised and battered doors.

Burberry used doors, painted a dramatic charcoal gray, to divide their window into a series of fashion vignettes. The accessories/coordinates are draped off hooks attached to the doors that are angled to make each "cubicle" an individual viewing stop. The doors also add a strong vertical line to the window composition.

It looks like moving day at Bendel's and whatever didn't fit into the moving van was put into this open back window to create a truly arresting composition. It seems to have everything—including the bathroom sink!

When you are too exasperated from trying to uncoil the damned coiled, twisted, knotted and maybe even leaky garden hose—don't despair. You can always just drop it into your display window—as is. That's what they did at Tiffany for their Spring/Summer trim. Refer back to Set the Scene for Summer and a look at how Bendel's used their knotted garden hose.

BURBERRY, New York, NY

TIFFANY & CO, New York, NY

HENRI BENDEL, Fifth Ave., New York, NY

FAÇONNABLE, Fifth Ave., New York, NY

Things that drip, drop, and cascade down from the ceiling are dangles and dangles can be subtle dividers in open back windows or just add shimmer/shine to a mannequin presentation where the danglers shower down around them.

Paper folded Origami birds are linked together into dangling chains to affect an interesting and textural background in the Façonnable window.

A shower of crystals adds interest to the Escada display as it partially "hides" the giant graphic on the rear wall.

ESCADA, E. 57th St., New York, NY

HENRI BENDEL,
Fifth Ave., New York, NY

HENRI BENDEL, Fifth Ave., New York, NY

At Bendel's, dangling strings of crystal beads, cappa shells, and wooden shapes are used to create a variety of settings. It is the iridescent mother of pearl shell disks that dangle in the Bendel open back window where the assembled sun-glassed mannequins strut out in their new light and white jeans. In a more Asian mood, the Anna Sui collection is partially framed with dangling strands of violet tinted glass beads and in another window, for a display of Asian-inspired garments, each abstract white mannequin is "framed" with a suspended curtain of wooden beads. The back wall is draped with a luxurious, gold colored satin fabric.

HENRI BENDEL, Fifth Ave., New York, NY

BERGDORF GOODMAN, Fifth Ave., New York, NY

Ribbons of silk, paper, plastic or even just strips of ripped fabric can also effectively dangle. Bergdorf plays the ribbon dangle card two ways. In one display the rear wall is covered with dozens upon dozens of lengths of assorted color and width ribbon streamers enhanced with an occasional bow—all in brilliant Technicolor—to match the colorful mix and match of casual clothes being presented. In a more formal manner, the ribbons—all pristine and elegant white—are manicured and controlled to affect a pull-back drape around the mannequin stepping forth in a red Armani gown.

BERGDORF GOODMAN, Fifth Ave., New York, NY

Paper streamers of assorted lengths and widths hang from the Saks Fifth Ave. ceiling and they are interspersed with "messages" printed on some of the dangles. They are announcing a "Trunk Showing" at the store. If the reader would look up to the ceiling, in the picture, he or she will see that the entire black painted ceiling is covered with a metal grid that facilitates the overall dangle experience.

SAKS FIFTH AVENUE, New York, NY

ANTHROPOLOGIE, Soho, New York, NY

Assorted cosmetics and toiletries come cascading down around the Bergdorf mannequin who is all set for the night. These night-time rejuvenators are cleverly arranged over the reclining figure that is surrounded by some exquisite bed linens.

Anthropologie, down in Soho, has used this effective way of bringing the garment into prominence while gently obliterating the view through the open back window. Swags of shredded muslin are pulled back for a theatrical effect but the "casual" approach to the pull back is certainly different from Bergdorf's approach with the Armani gown. This is totally informal!

BERGDORF GOODMAN, Fifth Ave., New York, NY

SAKS FIFTH AVENUE,
New York, NY

Simple blocks of color—lots of colors—can create an exciting background for color filled merchandise. Shown here are a selection of squares, rectangles and circles of assorted colors used creatively to enliven the merchandise presentation.

"Dot's Nice!" best describes Saks Fifth Avenue's display with the background covered with Technicolor dots. They could be colored light filters—or the shiny metal lids of paint cans or even just cut-out craft papers, but against the stark white wall and behind the white abstract mannequin in the neutral colored outfit—those dots send out a lively message. So do the rectangular, black spotted, colored panels in the other Saks window that create a strong horizontal line pattern. The horizontal board that holds the seated mannequin, up above, continues that line.

COACH, Fifth Ave.,
New York, NY

NORDSTROM, Chicago, IL

Nordstrom's window, like the Coach window, has a white grid filled with squares of color. Bendel's window is accentuated by the hanging rectangular panels of different colored Lucite. They back up the white shirted mannequins in the dark jeans and they also cut down on the view into the store through the open back window. The multicolored panels are repeated —with artwork—on the pedestals that affect a zig-zag line across the bottom of the window.

HENRI BENDEL,
Fifth Ave., New York, NY

DOTS NICE @ ANN TAYLOR

ANN TAYLOR, New York, NY

MANAGER OF VISUAL PRESENTATION: **Victor Johnson**

As Victor Johnson, Manager of Visual Presentation for Ann Taylor stores explains, "A strong apparel collection drawing on graphic prints, stripes and polka dots provided a wonderful starting point" for the early spring windows. He continues, "Our national window campaign featured gray and green 'poka dots' (translucent circles cut out and suspended from the ceiling) that reference one of the primary details in the fashion and marketing of the time period."

Shown here are the windows that appeared in various combinations throughout the U.S. In addition to the floating disks there were black and white photo blow-ups of models in the garments shown on the Ann Taylor mannequins. The images were printed on translucent fabric and suspended amidst the dots and the actual garments.

For the Madison Avenue flagship store blue and aqua garments were introduced along with the black and white garments and here the hanging dots were in a cool blue and gray—to further the fashion message.

MACY'S, Herald Square, New York, NY

Repetition, or making the same statement over and over again, can be boring or annoying, but repeating the same object over and over again can become a delightful design pattern.

A box is a box is a box except when the box—or square, or shape—is repeated over again in an interesting manner to make a design point. Macy's three framed messages mounted on white squares and each resting on an identical white plinth emphasizes "Seeds" and makes sense of the words spattered over the back wall. And it makes even more sense when this is one of many windows created for the store's annual flower show. In another window dimensional lotus blossoms are "framed" in identical frames that are regimentally lined up on the back wall.

MACY'S, Herald Square, New York, NY

GUCCI, Fifth Ave., New York, NY

Though the fashion images are all different, they are all treated the same way and hung in the same way and at the same height to make an interesting horizontal band across the Gucci window. Headless forms are shown in some of the outfits pictured on the graphic sheets.

Nordstrom's cubes all have the same artwork and all the cubes are mounted in vertical rows against black vertical panels. What adds interest and breaks up the possible "monotony" is that the faces of the cubes are highlighted with washes of different colors—in horizontal bands. The colors pick up the colors of the mannequin's outfit.

The same hosiery leg is repeated each time only at a higher level and each of the cylindrical platforms is the same only in different heights. The legs are each slightly askew for one another—again to break the monotony and in each instance Stuart Weitzman's fantasy shoes are raised up closer to the viewer's eye level—for a better look-see.

NORDSTROM, Chicago, IL

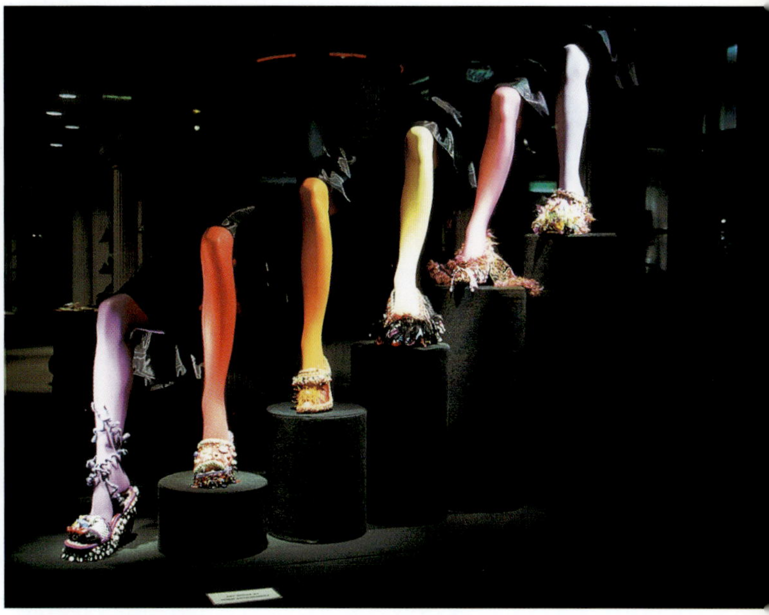

STUART WEITZMAN, Madison Ave., New York, NY

BLOOMINGDALE'S, Lexington Ave., New York, NY

Bloomingdale's doesn't mind repeating itself—especially if it helps to make a point. The dropped metal lamp shades are attracting and arresting. It is a neat and clever—and not very expensive—way to highlight the outfits on the abstract mannequins. In a swimwear window, the floor is covered with glass cylinders filled with blue water—as though these life-like mannequins were actually about to dive into any of these myriad miniature "pools."

Barneys is another one for restating the obvious—if it is fun, different and makes a selling point. The magazine covers are all the same and are set out on the back wall in a definite pattern of straight/angled/straight/angled, etc. The mannequin up front has turned her back on the viewers in the street and is telling them to look at the wall. It certainly doesn't hurt the "message" that we are afforded a view of the dress that is prominently displayed on all the magazine covers. In the Martin Grant display, the giant "snowflake" on the rear wall is a repetitive design made up of similar items to create the same look. The repetition continues down to the three dimensional clusters on the floor from which featured shoes are rising up.

BLOOMINGDALE'S, Lexington Ave., New York, NY

Saks does an artful job with the subtle repetition of baby bottles on the floor. They are "tying" daddy up with strings so that he can remember the feeding times. The oversized clock is there to remind him. What does this have to do with the fashions on display unless it is a Father's Day display? Who cares? We are looking at it and smiling—and that's what counts.

SAKS FIFTH AVENUE, New York, NY

BARNEYS NEW YORK,
Madison Ave., New York, NY

BARNEYS NEW YORK,
Madison Ave., New York, NY

BERGDORF GOODMAN, Fifth Ave., New York, NY

SAKS FIFTH AVENUE, New York, NY

So available—so expendaqble—so inexpensive! So infinite in its variety, colors, textures! Paper!! Paper on the roll, by the sheet; any color—smooth or textured—crimped or crumpled—cut or patched; there are myriad ways of using paper in display and here are some.

Bergdorf creatively patches pieces of paper with cream colored masking tape to affect this arresting patterned background. Note the dangling rolls of tape—still attached—adding a sense of immediacy to the action. More of the crumpled paper fills the floor and partially hides the mannequins' legs. In another window a typewriter (what's that?) is suspended way up in the tall window and gushes forth a long stream of crushed paper that falls to the floor and puddles around the headless mannequins.

As a background for the display of Zegna men's wear, the Saks Fifth Avenue window consists of panels of creased/crumpled white paper. It adds a sense of texture and contrast to the smooth, sleek garment on display.

BERGDORF GOODMAN, Fifth Ave., New York, NY

MARC O'POLO,
GUMS, Moscow, Russia

Barneys simply rolls out wide streamers of colored seamless paper to back up their Ralph Lauren collection of white separates. The swath of paper starts high up on the back wall—rolls down the back—across the floor and ends up in a curl at the window line.

At Marc O'Polo it is wrapping paper—kraft paper—that has been crumpled and shaped into the abstract forms behind the mannequins. The paper in neutral in color and complements the natural dried foliage and the clothes.

BARNEYS NEW YORK, Madison Ave., New York, NY

BERGDORF GOODMAN, Fifth Ave., New York, NY

Not just paper—but paper products like bags, stationery, and things made of paper.

Shopping bags take on a new meaning and provide an exciting textural quality in the Bergdorf windows where they seem to climb the heights in long vertical rows. Notice the change of color of the bags from one window to the next for a sense of variation and to better complement the garments up front. What a great effect for a clearance sale—with some bags up front spilling over-the-top with merchandise.

These letters will never get posted. They aren't even addressed but they do address the stationery available in Barneys Chelsea Passage. The envelops create a flap pattern on the rear wall and several dozen more are used to partially cover the skirt of the wicker figure on the left. The figure helps to bring attention to some of the items stocked in the highlighted area.

Sheets of construction paper are rolled—folded and even origami-ed into a textured white-on-white background for the Bendel window. Some of the cleverly folded and dimensional shapes appear as head-dressing on the white abstracts in the display of Hamish Morrow's clothes. In the store's open back window Henri Berndel's display staff creates giant orange colored pinwheels to attract viewers as well as "block" the opening. The pin wheels are motorized so that an invisible breeze keeps them spinning—and getting the attention of the passers by.

BARNEYS NEW YORK, Madison Ave., New York, NY

HENRI BENDEL,
Fifth Ave., New York, NY

IN THE SWIM @ THE BAY

THE BAY, Queen St., Toronto, ON, Canada
CREATIVE DESIGN MANAGER: **Ana Fernandes**
ISM DIRECTOR OF VISUAL PRESENTATION: **Denis Frenette**
PHOTOGRAPHER: **James Doiron**

If the time is right and if you are in the right place to dive in—you had better come prepared. The battery of windows that filled The Bay in Toronto certainly offered up all that would be needed and also showed how the outfits would look in the right ambiance.

At night, the windows took on an eerie, watery feeling—the feeling of being in an illuminated pool. The windows were flooded with aqueous aquas and watery blue tones. Suggestive stippling on the front glass of each window helped to underscore the underwater effect and that was enhanced by the schools of fish that surrounded some of the submerged mannequins. The mannequins were prepared with snorkeling masks and rubber flippers on their feet. As an amusing break of pattern, some of the mannequins floated near the top of the window rather than standing flipper firm in the sandy bottom of the make-believe sea.

RALPH LAUREN, Michigan Ave., Chicago, IL

Get on board a yacht—a cruise ship—a rowboat or a canoe and be off and sailing into warmer weather and sea, sand, sun and adventure.

Sails, ropes and a steering wheel (sort of) fill the Ralph Lauren windows along with the warm glow of sunlight. The sea-faring outfits are smart and ship-shape and definitely seaworthy. They are worn by sun-tanned stylized mannequins and on artfully draped traditional suit forms

It is "sails" at Searle where the abstracts are dressed mainly in black and white. The black and white ticking fabric that is used for the sail adds yet another pattern to the Op-Art window.

The paddles or oars lean against the shingled wall panel in Cole Haan's window to set the seaside scene. Note how the upright oars complement the vertical lines of the semi-abstract male mannequins in one window while the horizontal oars—in the other window—reinforce the lines of the shingles and the build-up of shingles that raise up the featured styles for viewing.

SEARLE, New York, NY

COLE HAAN, Fifth Ave., New York, NY

BROOKS BROS., Fifth Ave., New York, NY

There are clichés that are always available to visual merchandisers/display persons to create a Cruise & Resort ambiance such as lengths of bamboo, palm trees and palm fronds, tropical foliage, cabanas, striped awnings, stuccoed walls, and sea, sun, sky, sand and seashells. And then, too, there are visions of far-away lands and tropical islands in the sun.

How do you use these visual, trite and often overexposed props and make a difference? Shown here are some subtle, sly and often sophisticated versions of familiar symbols. St. John's window is soft and gentle and one can almost feel the soft breeze coming in from the sea to rustle the sea grass growing up from the sand that surrounds the dune fencing. The "paintings" serve as backgrounds for the two headless forms while the beach umbrella fills out the upper part of the white window.

Brooks Bros. window sets the scene for a holiday adventure to a tropic island. It provides the antique map—the giant palm tree—the canvas folding chairs and the traditional pull back curtains that will eventually keep out the buzzing and biting insects. The long drapes accentuate the double height windows of the store.

ST. JOHN BOUTIQUE, Fifth Ave., New York, NY

BANANA REPUBLIC, Fifth Ave., New York, NY

Banana Republic and E. Zegna go a bit architectural and abstract with their settings and the subtle touches of foliage reaffirm the resort message. Cole Haan's handbag rests in the cool shade of a striped awning—or nestles under a cabana—though still in the warm glow of tropical sunlight.

COLE HAAN, Fifth Ave., New York, NY

E. ZEGNA, Fifth Ave., New York, NY

BARNEYS NEW YORK, Madison Ave., New York, NY

Something Fishy? Well !! It certainly isn't smelly but the fish do bring along the scents and scenes of seaside activities.

A fabulous fish floats in the blue/green shadows of Barneys window to highlight the Rochas name and line of fashions. Constructed of rabbit wire over a skeleton of acrylic layers, the internally illuminated fish does create the underwater feeling. It is highlighted with square appliquéd "scales."

A pseudo-mosaic graphic background in blues and greens sets the scene as it takes over the rear wall of the Façonnable display window. Beach chairs and a palm tree starting its growth in a wicker basket flesh out the scene. On the graphic, stylized fish swim in and out of stylized mosaic patterned waves while underwater foliage grows up from the bottom of the make-believe sea.

FAÇONNABLE,
Fifth Ave., New York, NY

The all-white propped black window at Banana Republic makes a dramatic setting for the red, fuchsia and white separates being featured. A sailfish floats over the white chest that supports coral, starfish and seashells and the white bamboo-style chair completes the resort vignette imagery.

At Tiffany's the fishing is really good! The knotted rope ball and the Japanese screened fish—just pulled out of the sea—are complemented by the sand on the floor and the assorted colored glass bubble balls that bring the viewer's eye to the real Tiffany "baubles."

BANANA REPUBLIC,
Fifth Ave., New York, NY

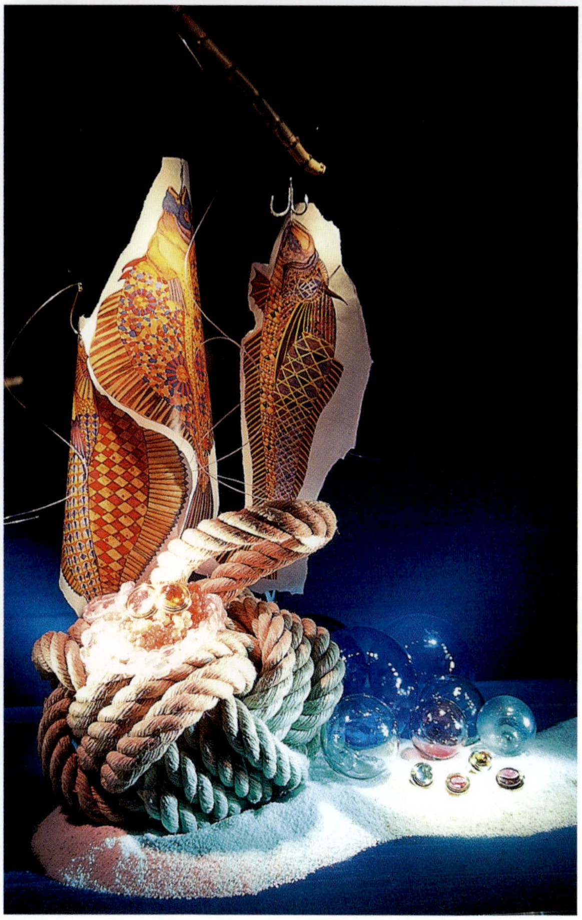

TIFFANY & CO., Fifth Ave., New York, NY

PLACE ALEXIS-NIHON, Montreal, QC, Canada
DESIGN: **Etalage B Display,** Montreal

When you are up in Quebec—in the middle of a cruel, bleak winter—it is warming and refreshing to come upon these bright and color filled—and stripped down—window displays. While outside the streets are snowy or slushy, behind the glass the symbols of sunny climes fill the windows and the fashions are made for swimming and sunning.

Place Alexis-Nihon is an upscale mall in Montreal and the designers at Etalage B Display, under the creative leadership of Constant Bibeau, created and installed these windows propped with decorative torso sculptures. Each window featured another strong colored background and symbols of the cruise/resort season

For the New Look shop in Quebec City, Etalage B Display had great fun with the brightly colored sea horses that—like the bikini clad mannequins—wore sporty sunglasses. These windows were designed by Marie-Eve Roy and Catherine Giroux working with M. Bibeau.

NEW LOOK, Quebec City, QC, Canada
DESIGN: **Etalage B Display,** Montreal, QC, Canada

BLOOMINGDALE'S, Lexington Ave., New York, NY

What says Cruise/Resort/Tropics/Faraway Islands/Cooling Breezes, etc. better than tall graceful swaying palm trees—or at least the many splendored types of palm fronds?

Bloomingdale's window is flushed with a warm, golden tropical light that turns the background into steaming red. Cooling off the scene are the palm tree and the ferns—and the green foliage entwined around the ropes that support the swing's seat that serves as an elevation for the mannequin.

Bendel's palm foliage and tree also serve to separate the boldly printed outfits up front from the activity in the store beyond. Also, the umbrella of palm fronds helps to set the "Exotic Escape" theme.

HENRI BENDEL, Fifth Ave., New York, NY

ESCADA, E. 57th St., New York, NY

RALPH LAUREN, Michigan Ave., Chicago, IL

Escada's jungle is wallpapered on three sides of the enclosed window and the lush, fabulous greenery creates a total environment for the semi-realistic mannequins. The white bamboo chairs suggest the tropics and also serve to bring some of the go-with accessories up off the floor and closer to the shopper's eye level.

Ralph Lauren's elegant window is white—as white as many of the garments being featured. White furniture, white frames, white flowers and white palm fronds surround the white semi-realistic mannequins in their pristine designer outfits. All together—the window created a blast of clean white glory on a gray street on a gray day in Chicago.

ANN TAYLOR, Stamford, CT

When you can't get the real thing or even the plastic version—there are always the prints and super photographic blow-ups. On these pages we show how a variety of shops relied on the "flat" version of palms to create a "dimensional" setting.

Ann Taylor used a blow-up of a tropical sunset as a background for their presentation of exotic print pattern garments and the go-with solid separates, while Chanel's realistic mannequins are all set for a day at the beach and the beach is suggested by the graphic panel printed on a translucent fabric. The panel sets the scene and also separates the window presentation from the store beyond the open back.

CRATE & BARREL, Madison Ave., New York, NY

CHANEL, Fifth Ave., New York, NY

Panels of photographic images of palm trees—suspended behind the colorful beach chairs, lanterns and patio ware—create the desired look for Crate & Barrel's summery look. To get shoppers into the right frame of mind to think "sunny climes" Bally's new bags and shoes are set out in the open boxes mixed in with the viridian/turquoise light boxes that fill the back of the window. The images on the light boxes are of sea, sky, sand and palm trees while in the self-illuminated cubes are the just right accessories to go with the setting.

BALLY, Fifth Ave., New York, NY

BAMBOOZLED @ ANN TAYLOR

ANN TAYLOR, Madison Ave., New York, NY
DIR. OF VISUAL DESIGN & PRESENTATION: **Victor Johnson**
PHOTOGRAPHY: **Kitty Cheung, Bryan Ellington**

In keeping with the chain's new attitude towards display, and under the able directorship of Victor Johnson, we are pleased to show Ann Taylor's summery promotion that was carried through in the New York area. The displays, shown here, are in the New York flagship store and bamboo was used along with other natural, textured materials in a variety of ways to set the scene for the mostly brown and white fashions that ranged from dress up to dress down casual—from street wear to pool side apparel.

The stylized white mannequins are realistically posed in groups that make the fashions easy to see—and coordinate. Chunks of bamboo of assorted diameters and lengths were either suspended from the ceiling to affect see-thru curtains in the open back windows or they were tied together to be used as risers, platforms or even seating for the mannequins. In other windows they were sliced and applied—on end—to create unusual plaques with textural interest.

What a way to go!! It is first class all the way: no passports required—no shots needed—no standing in line or having your bags scrutinized—no long, long hours cramped up in a plane. All you have to do to soak up the color, the thrill, the excitement of the South Seas is visit Lord & Taylor on Fifth Avenue in New York and walk the walk. L&T turned their front windows into a living museum with overscaled "paintings" of Gaugin's work in Tahiti as backgrounds for their summery line of clothes.

Once again Manoel Renha and his talented group have brought "art" to the "masses" and added "culture" to the commercial—and paid a compliment to the community by exposing them to "ART" but in the friendliest way. The gigantic "paintings" throb with color and the lush, lush foliage of the South Seas. The settings are rich, romantic and just right to complement the outfits worn by the realistic mannequins. Here is what the design team had to say about this set of windows:

"Our Gaugin windows were intended to evoke a lush tropicality with the warm earth and jewel-toned colors of the paintings echoing in the clothing and props. Gaugin's move to Tahiti towards the end

LORD & TAYLOR, Fifth Ave., New York, NY
DIVISIONAL VP OF VISUAL MERCHANDISING/SPECIAL EVENTS: **Manoel Renha**
PROJECT COORDINATOR/WINDOWS: **Nicole Moragne**

LORD & TAYLOR, Fifth Ave., New York, NY
DIVISIONAL VP OF VISUAL MERCHANDISING/SPECIAL EVENTS: **Manoel Renha**
PROJECT COORDINATOR/WINDOWS: **Nicole Moragne**

of the 19th century represented, for him, a flight from 'civilization' and a return to a more primitive and 'real' world. His painting's intense colors of this untamed nature brings to mind the proverbial Garden of Eden—an unspoiled paradise.

"We wanted to bring a little of this paradise to our summer windows. With hibiscus blossoms in their hair and the languid poses of women enjoying the sun, our mannequins display an array of swimsuits and summer dresses. Some, in white—punctuated with colorful embroidering or flowers—stand out against the backgrounds while others—in earth tones—mimic their painted counterparts. Translucent fabric panels screened with palm leaves in olive greens serve to further blur the boundaries between two and three dimensions."

HENRI BENDEL, Fifth Ave., New York, NY

Far away places are places we dream of. They are fantasies based on images we have seen in glorious Technicolor movies or greatly retouched photographs. They are Gauguin paintings or Shangri La—the ultimate in exotic places to run off to and escape from the stressful world. They are great places to go to for R & R.

Henri Bendel's window brings the exotic imagery to play in order to show fun, short-skirted fashions in one promotion and, in another, they utilize it to create a Zen-like mood for the Asian inspired casual wear by Christy Turlington. In the former: fans—folded and pleated—and ribbons dangle down in front of a fabric drape that wraps itself around the window. The fabric also is used for several of the separates featured in the window and worn by mirror finished abstract mannequins. A Chinese period throne adds to the fantasy of the setting. The Zen scene is richly lit in amber and gold light and the essence relies on the Ming tree and the floating bamboo branches—both encased or resting on clear plastic cubes—and the exotic top-knots on the otherwise hairless white abstract figures.

SAKS FIFTH AVENUE, (above and right)
New York, NY

BERGDORF GOODMAN, Fifth Ave., New York, NY

Bergdorf goes Asian for its inspiration but with fine Chinese artwork, cabinetry and accessories. All the props/furnishings come from an import/antique gallery and are on loan for use in the window. The "lender" is named on the front glass.

Saks also uses the far-away/exotic theme to promote the Oasis promotion. Shown here is a window featuring clothes in a North African setting and the beauty care products are lavishly set out on a mosaic tiled shelf that spans the window at the viewer's eye level and a giant reproduction of a Moorish tile design on the rear wall.

BURBERRY, E. 57th St., New York, NY

It is sea shells, sea horses, starfish and fish that all say seashore and cruise/resort.

Burberry's clear blue back wall is patterned with bleached starfish which helps create the setting for the abstract mannequins in their seagoing outfits.

Swarovski jewelry is shown on overscaled seashells that get the viewer's attention and in scale complement the precious pieces while still nodding to the selling season at hand. The cool aqua floor and build-ups are surrounded by dark mirrors that tend to enhance the pristine whiteness of the shells.

Fish take over the rich red/orange back wall in Coach's window that features abstracts in white outfits. The gold metallic fish swim amidst the gold "air bubbles" that tremble as they are extended off the back wall.

Tiffany's cool blue/green fish float in a blue undersea surrounding that suggests the deep blue sea. More fish are "caught" and held captive in the crewel basket from which strands of freshly caught pearls are trying to escape.

SWAROVSKI, Madison Ave., New York, NY

COACH, Fifth Ave., New York, NY

TIFFANY & CO., Fifth Ave., New York, NY

In another Tiffany window, bare branches—sprayed coral red—stand in for endangered branches of sea coral in this water logged setting. The gauzy white fabric that seems to float through the shadow box window suggests water or foam while blue/green glass beads are puddled on the sea's floor. The targeted light brings Tiffany's precious baubles into full view.

TIFFANY & CO., Fifth Ave., New York, NY

PLACE ALEXIS NIHON, Montreal, QC, Canada
INSTALLATION: **Etalage B Display,** Montreal, QC
CREATIVE DIRECTOR: **Constant Bibeau**
DESIGNERS: **Marie-Eve Roy, Guy Roberge**
PHOTOGRAPHY: **Courtesy of Etalage B Display**

The realistic mannequins in Place Alexis Nihon, an upscale mall in Montreal, QC, really did strip down for action but the action was set in a jungle. Using animal prints as the theme—giraffes, zebras leopards and other denizens of the wild—the display team at Etalage B Display combined the animal print fabrics with animal carvings, display props and such to carry out the Urban Jungle theme that featured black swimsuits and animal print suits and accessories. All together they created a set of unexpected looks for an "In the Swim" promotion—with a twist.

RÉGALO

BARNEYS NEW YORK,
Madison Ave., New York, NY

Take a picture—take lots of pictures—take tons of pictures: frame them—layer them—enlarge them—collage or montage them. Make them black and white or have them in full, brilliant color. They tell more than a thousand words and make interesting and/or exciting back wall treatments for display.

The designers of Barneys windows either have dozens of cameras fully loaded and ready to go—or they just love what they can do with them. They may be snapshots of moms provided by the store's employees for a Mother's Day promotion or just old family snaps filled with nostalgic details—or celebrity photos torn out of high fashion magazines or photos from new celebrity oriented books of photography. From full backgrounds and floor coverings to a few choice images highlighted or "framed" on colored panels of paper—Barneys does have a way with photographs.

BARNEYS NEW YORK, Madison Ave., New York, NY

LIMITED EXPRESS,
W. 34t St., New York, NY

ANN TAYLOR,
Madison Ave., New York, NY

More examples of photographs used to cover back walls and help promote the product being featured up front. The almost neutral blue/black and flesh tinted photos at Limited Express carry trough the denim/black/navy story while the blast of color filled photos actually anticipate the brightness of the yellow in the Ferragamo display.

There is something neat and orderly about the photo arrangements at Ann Taylor and Saks Fifth Ave. Where the emphasis on the picture arrangement is horizontal at Ann Taylor—there is a strong vertical presentation at the Saks Fifth Avenue display. The line in the composition helps to tell something about the merchandise offer.

The same few photos of the same (or similar) garment is played over and over again in a carefree presentation in Promod's window. The scattered, diagonal line-filled background is tempered by the neat and orderly laydown of the folded garments and coordinates up front.

FERRAGAMO, Fifth Ave., New York, NY

PROMOD, Budapest, Rumania

SAKS FIFTH AVENUE, New York, NY

BLOOMINGDALE'S, Lexington Ave. New York, NY

HENRI BENDEL, Fifth Ave., New York, NY

Summer means getting out into the open—getting out under blue skies—enjoying the sunshine—going al fresco. To show off summery fashions, what better way is there to do it than to bring the out-of-doors into the window setting.

Bloomingdale's set the scene: an outdoor café probably in the swinging east 60s and part of the store's neighborhood. Here it is "see and be seen." It is OK to gawk as you sip your caffe latte. The lightweight outdoor tables and chairs add depth and dimension as well as elevations for the display of "go-with" accessories while the background drawing adds the charm.

The picnic table and benches, the picket fence and flowering bushes in Henri Bendel's open back window all suggest a back yard scene. The snaking water hose adds a touch of humor—and realism—to the scene.

BROOKS BROTHERS,
Fifth Ave., New York, NY

COACH, (above and above right), Madison Ave., New York, NY

The table and chairs that are used in the Brooks Brothers window along with the striped tent, the green grass mat flooring and the tennis rackets all suggest a Hampton's/Country Club setting: a place where you "dress up" to "dress down" as you enjoy a day away from the city.

Coach takes on summer with these two sketchy scenes. In one the abstract linear tree serves to hold the swing that, in turn, supports the mannequin while artwork provides the clumps of grass and the flight of the bumble bee. Summer Chic sets the stylized white mannequin against an outdoor patio setting that is artfully sketched in black and gray on white and highlighted with red and blue. The red touches pick up the red in the Coach shoes and bag.

THE BAY, Queen St., Toronto, ON, Canada
CREATIVE DESIGN MANAGER: **Ana Fernandes**
ISM DIRECTOR VISUAL PRESENTATION: **Denis Frenette**
PHOTOGRAPHER: **James Doiron**

Even if your passport is out of date and you didn't bring your walking shoes, you can still get the feeling of being away—far, far away—from the noise, traffic and hubbub of downtown Toronto. The Bay broke with this battery of vacation windows to show off a vast array of new summer into fall fashions in their Queen Street windows.

The "stamp" that appeared on the front glass proclaimed "Summer Vacations" highlighted by a sun motif. The background of each window was a giant blow-up of a colored post card-like view of some favorite holiday destination and then a few, well selected props were added to create a dimensional feeling to the scene.

The five scenes shown here highlight some of the top vacation sites in Canada, The vignettes cross the continent from Niagara Falls and the fishing villages of New Brunswick to a Calgary "round-up" in the West that serves as the raison d'etre for a display of jeans. The Bay did not ignore the European charm and flavor of Quebec City which is represented by an outdoor café with an architectural balustrade, lamp light and some lightweight outdoor furniture. To show that this was a trans-Canada holiday—a "dotted line," on the front glass, marks the route and also highlights each destination.

Summer Vacation
MOUNT ROYAL, QC

Summer Vacation

BERGDORF GOODMAN MEN'S, Fifth Ave., New York, NY

Whether it is indoors or outdoors, the Sporting Life does make an attractive, active and fun lifestyle setting for casual fashions.

In the light—assorted, multi-colored bulbs for light—Bergdorf's Men's window definitely yells out "Tilt!" The off kilter angle of the pin ball machine creates a sense of movement and action that helps to animate the headless, motionless forms. The "excitement" of the game is further accentuated by the bombardment of the colored lights throughout the window.

You might never realize it but Samuel & Sons does not sell croquet equipment, but they do make use of the hoops, the mallets and the balls to promote the varied selection of fabric braids and decorative edgings—"passementerie." The green grass mat below and the flowering boughs above create an outdoors setting and bring the viewer to the colorfully bound and trimmed croquet equipment.

SAMUEL & SONS, New York, NY

GANT, Fifth Ave. New York, NY

Riding the surf—in style and in full, glorious color. In the Gant display the brightly colored and patterned surfboards tie in with the sharp, primary colored clothes worn by the headless forms. Men's and women's wear are coordinated in this splashy display that is "finished" with canvas chairs and Gant bags. Adding to the sizzle is the neon tubing outlining each surfboard which makes them decorative props rather than the real thing.

At the Zegna Boutique, surfboard-shaped panels of white plastic and mirror are used to create visual dividers between the smart, sophisticated outfits shown on headless mannequins. In both instances, the side walls are covered with colored light boxes that add an attraction to each window. This is "surfin' with style" and the shape is more important than the "real thing." The repetition of the graceful vertical elements adds a sense of prestige and value to the merchandise.

ZEGNA, Fifth Ave., New York, NY

BLOOMINGDALE'S, Lexington Ave., New York, NY

Denims, today, can be used to "dress down" or "dress up" for almost any occasion. They can be—and are—seen out in the woods, on the playing field, roughing it, shopping in town or with a tuxedo jacket and open dress shirt making it down the red carpet to an award ceremony or to the opera.

The cluttered, prop filled Bloomingdale window makes the shopper stop and question what's going on. It is retro-message glorifying and drenched in the Hippie movement and the music of the early 1970s. In another window stuffed and stacked full of denim jeans, the message in the window is about the Lucky Brand Foundation and the "peace power" symbol of those rambunctious days helps to bring the past into the present.

BLOOMINGDALE'S, Lexington Ave., New York, NY

Henri Bendel capitalizes on the success and the buzz of the *Desperate Housewives* TV series as the draw for their Denim/ Jean collection. The assorted mops, pails and cleaning equipment enhance the "housewives" theme while the anything but shy and retiring mannequins are no longer "desperate" as they revel in showing off what they are wearing.

Swinging to the other end of the dress code spectrum is the Diesel display with the jean wearing "gentleman" with his favorite dog—framed in gilt and set in a lush, plush super upscale setting. These are jeans with tradition that can go and do go anywhere at any time.

The Levi's display is denim/jeans right out of the corral and onto Michigan Avenue in Chicago. The rustic wood frame and structure support an overload of assorted jeans and go-with shirts just stacked and racked up to point out the vast selection available inside. Two headless mannequins wear some of the Levi's jeans and they stand in front of a blow-up of a Levi's logo graphic.

HENRI BENDEL, Fifth Ave., New York, NY

DIESEL, Lexington Ave., New York, NY

LEVI'S, Michigan Ave., Chicago, IL

THE BAY, Toronto, ON, Canada
CREATIVE DIRECTOR: **Ana Fernandes**
ISM DIRECTOR VISUAL PRESENTATION: **Denis Frenette**
PHOTOGRAPHER: **James Doiron**

Blue and jeans go together like ham and eggs or fish and chips. Think blue and you get the classic jean. The Bay, in Toronto, played with that concept in two promotions: "Thinking in Shades of Blue" and "Code Blue."

Lightweight, translucent plastic forms float, fly and generally "take off" in assorted blue colored jeans when they hear "Code Blue." The all-white corner window featured the theme, in blue letters, on the rear wall and the blue bull's eye that radiated the call on the floor. All over the white floor there are blue flashing lights with blue electric wires snaking over the all white space. The forms, fitted with parachute harnesses, are making an emergency drop at the assigned spot in answer to the Code Blue call.

In "Thinking in Shades of Blue," the same translucent forms were used and here the all white environment was washed with blue light. Adding to the attraction was again the use of electric bulbs. Here, the cool blue lamps are glowing atop the heads of the figures adding an almost surreal "Alien" quality to the displays. The jeans on display run the gamut from pale washed out, pastel blue to deep, dark inky blues and with the upper parts of the bodies almost invisible—the attention goes to the denim covered lower halves.

HARVEY NICHOLS, London, UK
VISUAL MERCHANDISING CONTROLLER: **Janet Wardley**
WINDOW DISPLAY MANAGER: **Laura O'Connor**
PROPS: **Icon Studio** and **Make Stuff**
PHOTOGRAPHY: **Michael Taylor**

For anyone who has not been to London—let me explain. Knightsbridge is an area where commerce, culture and class all come together. Harrods sits on Brompton Rd. and just two streets away—and where Brompton St. meets Sloane St. is Harvey Nichols with display windows wrapping around two sides of the building. Head down Sloane St. towards Kings Row—another shopping area—and you will see many top designer brand boutiques lining both sides of this posh, upscale street. If there is any place in London where a store's brand image makes a difference—this is it!

We are pleased to show on these pages some of the really exciting and brand enhancing images produced in the Harvey Nichols windows where noted designer fashions are set forth. Janet Wardley is the store's visual merchandising controller and she is ably assisted by Laura O'Connor who is the window display manager. We start our review with "Faded White."

Eerie, dramatic, theatrical, attention-getting! These windows tell a story but the script is the one the viewer makes up for herself. Soft, muted creamy whites and cool whites fill the background and color the props. If ever there were "found"—items used with flair and imagination—this is it. A stacking of old, mismatched chairs and a weathered, rickety table are used to elevate the mannequins in HN's very tall windows. "Antique"—but more likely "discarded"—period furniture and wispy sheer curtains almost suggest "A Streetcar Named Desire" setting for the casually dressed pair. Add details like leaded glass windows in beaten-up old frames or a door shedding layers of paint onto a floor of broken bits and pieces of lumber, faux textured walls and shredded lace hangings and it all adds up to a romantic, semi-Gothic, bodice-ripping set of intriguing windows.

BERGDORF GOODMAN, Fifth Ave., New York, NY

HENRI BENDEL, Fifth Ave., New York, NY

DKNY, Madison Ave., New York, NY

THE BAY, Toronto, ON, Canada

Along with fall comes Back to School—back to books and back to dormlife. At Bergdorf it is the old, wooden filing cabinets that are used to create the desired ambiance for "What to Wear on Campus"—and it all appears to be filed under "Fashion Approved." The pulled out, open file drawers not only add planar interest but serve as platforms for some of the fashion accessories.

Books!! That is what it is all about at DKNY and Henri Bendel. At Bendel, it is a balancing act as to how to hit the books and still be in fashion. The realistic mannequin appears to have finally got it right, but the books scattered on the floor say that it took several tries. DKNY has lined their entrance wall with a "library" of books; all screened on wallpaper and dimensionalized with an occasional bookshelf that is used to support some of DKNY's fashion-forward accessories. The study group, in the main open-back window, is dressed as though they are ready to forsake their books for a night on the town. So much for hitting the books!!

At The Bay, it is all about dorm life and all that it might take to "move in" and be ready to live a life away from home as though you never left home. Some of the "things" that will make life away livable are displayed on pedestals and tables in these bright and colorful windows.

Fall, at The Bay in Toronto, is a time for mystery, romance, elegance—and dressing up. In window after window, the display team created settings opulent and eye-catching—rich in red velour, flocked wallpapers, ornate gilded frames surrounding classic portraits, twisted and elaborate crystal chandeliers, old furniture and even older books, black crows, grouse, antlers and gnarled black lacquered branches that were melded into eerie and forest-like frames around each setting.

The surreal settings were full of intrigue, interest, wonder and detail and each elicited another mood or feeling. The female mannequins all were topped with white, cotton-candy wigs that, with the twisted branch prosceniums, tied all the different scenes into a cohesive, shopper-stopping experience.

THE BAY, Toronto, ON, Canada
CREATIVE DESIGN MANAGER: **Ana Fernandes**
DIRECTOR VISUAL PRESENTATION: **Denis Frenette ISM**
PHOTOGRAPHY: **James Doiron**

BURBERRY, Madison Ave, New York, NY

HICKEY FREEMAN, New York, NY

BANANA REPUBLIC, Fifth AVE., New York, NY

ANTHROPOLOGIE, Soho, New York, NY

H&M, W. 34th St., New York, NY

Whether it is a single birch tree or a mini forest of white and gray striped striplings, the bare branches—the leafless look—all set the scene for fall into winter.

Burberry combined a cluster of birch trees up front and backed them up with a "rendered" forest in soft focus on the back wall. Individual trees seem to pop up from the floor that is covered with drifts of puffy, glistening snow that pouts the "br-r-r" into the outerwear fashions being shown.

At Hickey Freeman, the paper-thin bark has been stripped off the birch trees and the feeling of fall permeates the men's fashion presentation. Some of the bark still adheres to the tree while more is scattered over the floor to further the autumnal look.

A single bare, leafless tree and a street lamp is all it took to suggest that fall had arrived at the Banana Republic. Though some leaves are scattered on the floor, the lifestyle photo that is centered in the composition suggests that changes in weather are on the way.

Twigs, branches and snow come together in the wreath/frame that encircles the dressform in the Anthropologie window. Since it is a large, open-back window, the circular frame serves to focus the viewer's eye on the garment being displayed on the form in the center of the focal "bull's eye."

H&M sets their scene with a backlit photo that has been divided into nine squares. The scene is of bare branches with some tenacious leaves still holding on—reluctant to give into the winds of autumn. The male and female mannequins are dressed for the chilly days that are blowing their way.

BLOOMINGDALE'S, Lexington Ave., New York, NY

BERGDORF GOODMAN, Fifth Ave., New York, NY

Rough pieces of wood—battered and bruised by exposure to water, wind and sand—or smooth, slick, sawed and shaved wood in planks, plinths or piers have the feel, the texture, the touch and the essence of fall.

Saks Fifth Avenue and Bloomingdale's greeted the season with chunks of textured driftwood picked up at the seashore or off withering trees. While Bloomingdale's designers opted for hanging pieces of the driftwood from hempen string to create a unique "forest" for their stylized white mannequins to stroll through, Saks contrasted bits of sawed off, rough-barked timber with smooth background panels. One of the pieces serves as a platform for a single, elegant strip sandal.

At Bergdorf the pieces of lumber are nailed together to form clean, clear pine wood "trees." Like children's drawings, the naive, simple, stick-drawings-in-dimension work to affect an arresting setting for men's fall outfits.

SAKS FIFTH AVENUE, Fifth Ave., New York, NY

SAKS FIFTH AVENUE, Fifth Ave., New York, NY

Saks also created its own forest of lumber. Here the "trees" are actually 2x4 lengths of lumber hanging from above. In another window, pieces of finished 2x2, 2x4 and 4x4 lumber are attached perpendicular to the back panel that carries a blow-up of an ad for Youth Dew. Quite a contrast!

SAKS FIFTH AVENUE, Fifth Ave., New York, NY

ST. JOHN BOUTIQUE, Fifth Ave., New York, NY

OR the Leaves of Fall. Gold, orange, red or brown—realistic or stylized—life size or humungous—leaves are synonymous with fall and fall fashions.

At St. John, metallic gold leaves attached to a metal vine partially frame the realistic mannequin in the black and white outfit. The oversized leaves and the metallic finish add a sense of elegance and refinement to an already class outfit.

The layers of cut-out brown paper that create a series of receding arches or frames around the dress form in the Anthropologie window simulate branches of leaves even though the cut-outs are not true leaf shapes. The progression from the layer against the glass to the last one several feet back in the open back window create a dramatic sense of depth and perspective for the featured garment.

ANTHROPOLOGIE, Soho, New York, NY

TIFFANY & CO., Fifth Ave., New York, NY

Fortunoff faces the fall season and the fall/winter weddings with this creative effort where the mannequins are decorated and dressed in leaves. Traditional fall colors and leaves are used on the rear figure while the "bride's" gown is tier after tier of white leaves. The pedestal on the left is trimmed with over scaled leaves to follow through on the theme.

Paper leaves and papier mache tree branches fill the Tiffany shadow box windows with the essence of fall. Colored lights enhance the autumnal look while warm spots pick out the precious gold, carnelian and malachite jewelry.

FORTUNOFF'S,
Fifth Ave., New York, NY

BERGDORF'S STORE FOR MEN,
Fifth Ave., New York, NY

The leaves fall off something! The bare branches—the nude trees—the skeletal forest—that is what is left when the leavers fall but they are enough to set the season's look.

Bergdorf created its own forest of bare birch trees set against a background of raw 4x4s, 2x4s and other trimmed pieces of lumber. Altogether they create a great, neutral but highly textured background for the neutral colored semi-casual men's outfits.

A cold, cold and very naked forest of tree trunks and branches serves as a background for Cole Haan's leather coat shown on a suit form. To present some of Cole Haan's other leather accessories, a platform has been constructed and faced with numerous split logs still covered with rough bark. It is chilly and neutral and sets the temperature for the warm and warming products.

COLE HAAN, Fifth Ave., New York, NY

STEUBEN GLASS, Fifth Ave., New York, NY

At Steuben Glass birch tree saplings are bare, bare branches are set onto a grass and product covered piece of lumber that still wears its rough outer edge of bark as a decorative hem. Colorful "mushrooms" and "toad-stools" accentuate the clear crystal items that have been elevated for better viewing by the shoppers on the street.

Tiffany combines neutral colored birch logs with colorful peacock feathers in their shadow box windows. Ceramic fall fruits and vegetables in a pewter finish add a seasonal touch to the presentation of the jewelry being featured.

TIFFANY & CO., Fifth Ave., New York, NY

GUCCI, Fifth Ave., New York, NY

Wood—lumber or timber—finished or unfinished—smooth or rough—vertical or horizontal—whatever! They all say fall or autumn without resorting to the traditional leaves, flowers or the usual colors.

Gucci creates a strong horizontal pattern in its window with a series of logs lined up one atop the other and with pieces gouged out to reveal the inner surface color and textures against the darker color and rougher grain of the exterior. A single shoe and handbag are featured in the neutral ambiance. In another Gucci set up there is a build-up of wooden boards interrupted by shorter boards that step out as they build upwards. The cantilevered boards become shelves or display platforms for the Gucci shoes and bags. Here, too, the display glows with a warm, rich golden light that warms not only the natural wood but the product display as well.

Bloomingdale's window is filled with exciting, dynamic lines that counteract the elegant vertical line of the realistic mannequins. The background/foreground consist of slabs of dark stained wood "jack-strawed" to frame the beige colored clothing. The diagonals create a sense of excitement that dramatically enhances the garment presentation.

Straw may be related to barns and horses but it also works as a fall texture. Bales of the golden dried stalks are piled up in Steuben Glass's window and with their rich color and texture, the bales serve as risers and platforms to elevate the featured pieces of crystal for easy viewing. Just as the straw contrasts with the smooth glass, so does

BLOOMINGDALE'S,
Lexington Ave., New York, NY

the elegant chaise/chair contrast with the rural setting and the rope that is twisted around it. A real surprise for the traditional Steuben viewer/shopper.

The wire sculptured leaf that dominates Bloomingdale's sun drenched back wall is all texture. A construction of rods, wire, and nails heads on a terra cotta colored leaf shaped panel, the unit blends with the rich golden colored rear wall and the mostly earthy colored garments on the realistic mannequins. The single turquoise dress stands out in the composition.

STEUBEN GLASS, Fifth Ave., New York, NY

BLOOMINGDALE'S, Lexington Ave., New York, NY

BERGDORF STORE FOR MEN, Fifth Ave., New York, NY

Good anytime and every time one wants to make a class statement. Classics have withstood the test of time and trends—and are all about good taste, fine quality and enduring looks. Usually—to interpret or introduce the "new classics" we refer back to the classical arts and architecture of Greece and Rome.

Bergdorf goes classic with a vengeance. A classic bust on a pedestal on the left looks on in bewilderment at the new "classic" motorbike—and the assortment of men's wear. The theme is all about Italian design and style and the classic bust backed up by the photo montage of things Italian sets the scene for the imported featured outfits.

Shakespeare may not have been Greek or Roman but his works are classics and thus the giant bust of the poet/ playwright is backed up by hundreds of classics in the forms of books. Busts of other classic authors appear amid the books. And all that to present the seasons "Casual Classics" at Bergdorf's.

ELMIRA EYEWEAR,
Elmira, ON
DESIGN: **Melissa Reitzer**

Cole Haan uses the classic architectural arcade to create the setting for the men's and women's outfits. A renaissance patterned background covers the rear wall and complements the arches in the foreground.

A bust of Venus now sprouts a luxurious coiffeur of ferns and feathers in Tiffany's window. The stark and dramatic black and white window is highlighted with accents of golden light and the featured jewelry adorns the neck of the classic bust.

Melissa Reitzer really went classic with her display for Elmira Eyewear. Using a variety of classic and neo-classic columns, pedestals and urns—all white—and a floor covered with white moss and baby's breath, she created a very fashionable display for several featured frames. Soft, pastel green drapes artfully add diagonal lines into the composition which is mainly vertical—except for the toppled over columns.

TIFFANY & CO., Fifth Ave., New York, NY

COLE HAAN, Fifth Ave., New York, NY

BERGDORF GOODMAN, Fifth Ave., New York, NY

BERGDORF GOODMAN, Fifth Ave., New York, NY

What is a more natural "go-with" to complement Back to School or the fashions and events that come in with autumn than the Classic theme? Greek and Roman motifs from antiquity—to the writings of Shakespeare or any re-readable book up to the early 20th century—music that is still played—all *classics*. A classic has lasting qualities; it is usually refined, elegant, polished and finished—and undiminished by time or actually enriched by it. Here are some "classic" displays.

At Bergdorf, classic Georgian architectural elements, motifs and decoratives are treated in new and different ways to serve as settings for Fall fashions. Josiah Wedgwood's classic blue and white palette is teamed up with Adam's late 18th century dictionary of classic motifs is clever assemblages that incorporate and envelop the mannequins. Note how one gown-clad mannequin stands atop a floating base enhanced with a rosette design.

Bloomingdale's plays the Classics as well but with fluted columns and Corinthian caps. There is even a pedestal for a mannequin to stand upon to assume a classic pose. Classic Roman statuary—white plastercasts—also further the elegant, timeless quality of the white gowns on the realistic mannequins. The scene seems to have been pulled right out of Figure Drawing class 101. A perfect switch.

BLOOMINGDALE'S, Lexington Ave., New York, NY

BLOOMINGDALE'S, Lexington Ave., New York, NY

BERGDORF GOODMAN, Fifth Ave., New York, NY

If music be the soul of fashion—as it often appears to be at Bergdorf Goodman—then play on! We have on numerous occasions shown eye-catching, enticing and enigmatic uses of music and musical instruments in Bergdorf Goodman's windows. Whether real or fantasized, they are used to prop Bergdorf's designer brand fashions.

Super, super violins and horns turn the headless forms into lilliputian figures; almost delicate miniatures in comparison to the size of the overscaled instruments. And yet, when comparing the dresses to the sheets of music that paper the back wall of these very tall windows, the scale is just right and as it should be.

Silhouettes of musical instruments—all cut from sheets of music composition paper—mounted on stained plywood panels create a unique setting for the de la Renta dresses shown on the headless forms up front.

For a black and white promotion what is as black and white as musical notes printed on a sheet? Here, the Gaultier black and white outfits appear in an all-white ambiance and the rear wall carries a collage of bits and pieces of overscaled sheet music and a mix of musical instruments sprayed black and white as well as prints of the same instruments. Note how black shoes and fashion accessories are integrated into the collage.

Music is an anytime, all-the-time kind of theme that can be adapted to any season, holiday or event. There is a song for every occasion and as shown here—so many different ways to play that tune.

BERGDORF GOODMAN, Fifth Ave., New York, NY

ST. JOHN, Fifth Ave., New York, NY

Black and white—night and day—light and dark. Contrasts! Complements! Yin and Yang! It is the opposite that counts and the sharp contrast of white on black or black on white that really gets the viewer's attention. Whether the garments are all white or white trimmed in black—or the gowns are black and set against white backgrounds—it is all about contrast.

St. John's window features a black and white print dress and a black skirt topped with a black top pierced to reveal the white beneath. The realistic mannequins are dramatically posed against a stark white background where giant shiny black disks tumble down to meet the inflated black balls on the floor.

Robert Ellis's realistic mannequins wear gowns in black, white and black and white. The window designer, Keith Dillion, has selected a background of dimensional pinwheel-like flowers—white on white—to set off the three outfits

ROBERT ELLIS, W. Hollywood, Los Angeles, CA

COLE HAAN,
Fifth Ave., New York, NY

CHANEL,
Fifth Ave., New York, NY

Cole Haan's background is a Mondrian pattern of black, silver and white rectangles—some dimensionalized—and it serves to set off the black, white and gray separates in the foreground on headless forms. The Cole Haan accessories—shoes and bags—appear to either side raised up on cubes for better viewing.

Chanel plays up a white on black print dress—all accessorized in white—against an architectural setting of dimensional white frames. A simple Chanel handbag pops out from the contrasting setting. In another display, the designer's name is spelled out in giant white dimensional letters while a Parisian street scene—in black and white—fills in the background and still manages to get the Chanel name up over the big letters. The mannequin wears a white suit accented in black with black accessories to keep the contrasting theme going.

GUCCI, Fifth Ave., New York, NY

ADRIENNE VITTADINI, Fashion Show, Las Vegas, NV

Against a background of cutout ellipses of assorted sizes—nested and repeated over and over again till they created an overall pattern on the white back wall—Gucci's white gowns were shown on headless forms.

The Adrienne Vittadini's open back window showed a selection of mix and match black and white separates and accessories in a stark white setting. A black and white graphic plus some patterned garments hanging in the window furthered the black and white theme.

TIFFANY & CO., Fifth Ave., New York, NY

ROBINSONS, Fashion Show, Las Vegas, NV

Robinsons' in-store display of printed black and white fabric bags and accessories had a blow-up of the printed design as a background for the bags shown on the glass shelves. Black and white outfits—on the top shelf—accented with the featured bags told the story from a distance.

Tiffany & Co. went polka-dotty in black and white with backgrounds and floors of their shadow box windows covered in the contrasting duo with classic white column caps adding a sense of dignity—and class to the displays of gift items. The white feather boa added another touch of lightness—and frivolity to the product display.

SCHREIBMEISTER, Munich, Germany
DISPLAY DESIGNER: **Gert Muller**

SCHREIBMEISTER, Munich, Germany
DISPLAY DESIGNER: **Gert Muller**

Gert Muller, the display director at Schreibmeister in Munich is not only a "quick change" artist with complete window changes every two or three weeks, but he is clever at promoting small and similar products like pens, pencils, pads and stationery in the same confined open back space.

Muller manages to get attention for his products through the use of strong dynamic patterns and with color—or the lack of color. He seems to often switch from a color or color family to a very stark black and white combination that sort of cleanses the palette before the next onset of a color promotion.

We have selected some of the windows Gert Muller produced during the year where he has used strong pattern and stark black and white to announce the fact that there has been a window change and something new is on view. Stripes, checkerboard, diagonals, dots or stars—all make strong statements in the allotted space. The back panel that carries the décor serves to separate the small products up front from the vast store interior beyond. It is also interesting to note that the sharp neutral palette isn't confined to any one event or time of the year; it can, and does, work any time to shake things up and announce a change of theme or color promotion.

SAKS FIFTH AVENUE, New York, NY

What's black and white and usually "read" all over? Well, in the past—nothing said black and white as well as newspapers and newsprint but now that color is creeping into the daily news—it may not be as obvious.

Saks Fifth Avenue covered the rear wall with newspapers: folded newspapers overlapped to create a wonderful, shadow-filled and textured wall treatment. Stacks of the newspapers fill in the floor—tumbling, building, falling or whatever to tie together the rear wall and the floor right up to the window. The white mannequin with black wig and makeup wears a smart black suit/dress and stands out theatrically from her surroundings.

Crumpled, tossed away newspapers are scattered on the floor of the American Eagle window while the headless forms—some floating—are busy catching up on their reading. The big news is "CLEARANCE" and those screaming headlines can be seen over and over again in this amusing sale display that appeared in the Cobbs County Mall in Georgia.

Keith Dillion, the display designer for Robert Ellis boutique in W. Hollywood had "FALL NEWS" to spread in his window. To tell his red and black merchandise story, Dillion filled the foreground with neatly organized and stacked piles of papers tied chic-ly with black ribbons. The background panel is a collage of newspaper sheets enhanced with a black Greek key motif and FALL NEWS printed over it. White stylized mannequins complement the red and black outfits.

AMERICAN EAGLE, Cobbs County Mall, Georgia

ROBERT ELLIIS, West Hollywood, Los Angeles, CA

BARNEYS NEW YORK, Madison Ave., New York, NY

BARNEYS NEW YORK, Madison Ave., New York, NY

The dressform is a cliché: it speaks of designer clothes, high fashion ateliers—of things made to order. It also is—in some instances—a relic—a symbol of the past and the shapes and forms of bygone eras. Here we present how designers have used traditional—and not so traditional—dressforms to get the fashion message across.

Barneys creates a parade of dressforms—past, present and futuristic—in this color-filled window that features the print splattered designs of Junya Watanabe. It is almost like a "history of body forms" done tongue-in-cheek. In a more dramatic mood the design team at Barneys made effective use of black wire dress forms of assorted sizes, shapes and poses to present a collection of red and black garments in a coolly-lit white window.

The heroic scaled graphic of the red corset on Henri Bendel's white wall is seen again in the three dimensional red plush mache dress forms mixed in with the clothes by Sarah Berman.

The bare, as is, dress form serves as a mass and a focal point in the Louis Vuitton window of fashion accessories. A Vuitton scarf is twisted around the form's neck while the other accessories appear at the base. Here, the dress form is synonymous with "designer."

In Ripley's silverware display, Karina Barhumi makes clever use of the suit forms that are finished in a heavily textured fabric. With the addition of black bow ties and black cummerbunds they become waiters serving up a selection of Italian imported cookware for the people in Lima.

RIPLEYS, Lima, Peru

LOUIS VUITTON, Stockholm, Sweden

HENRI BENDEL, Fifth Ave., New York, NY

MARSHALL FIELD'S State St., Chicago, IL

ROBERTO CAVALLINI, Las Vegas, NV

Framed or unframed, mirrors can be tricky, clever, amusing, reflective—and troublesome. If not angled and lit properly they can cause more confusion than solve any presentation problems. But, they can be very rewarding in creating numerous views and a variety of viewing angles on the same garment.

At Marshall Field's, on State St. in Chicago, the framed and unframed slivers of mirror—cut with angles and oblique lines—add a tremendous sense of excitement and action to the display of active sportswear. In addition to all the diagonal lines, it is the reflections—the new and changing imagery—as the shopper walks by that provides that extra dollop of stimulation to these cool displays.

Also depending upon the movement outside the window are the large framed mirrors in the Roberto Cavallini window in Las Vegas. The mirrors are set at an angle to each other so that the viewer not only sees all sides of the featured garments but different angles as he or she moves by.

ROBERT ELLIS, Studio City, CA
DESIGN: **Keith Dillion**

ST. JOHN, Fifth Ave., New York, NY

St. John's classic outfit gets an additional sparkle from the mosaic of mirrored rectangles set into the back wall. The beveled edges catch and reflect light and movement while the larger image of the dressed mannequin is replayed on the fractured back panel.

The pier mirror shaped somewhat like a Gothic window frame serves to show off the front of the mannequin's gown while replaying the theme—"Reflections of You." As a followup to the previous "Framed" entry, notice the frames used on the fabric covered wall panel.

ST. JOHN, Fifth Ave., New York, NY

Mirrors are usually on the wall and mostly in one piece but drop them—break them—fracture or split them and it won't necessarily bring you seven years of bad luck. It could turn into some sensational reflective and reflecting window displays as those shown here.

St. John isn't afraid of the broken mirror or even Friday the 13th. The fragmented mirror is "reassembled" to give the viewer on the street a multi-angled look at the whole garment—front and back. The pierces are patched together on the rear wall, down to the floor—under the mannequins and end up at the glass line.

In The Limited's window, the mirrored squares are clipped together to create a semi-open screen that serves as a divider in the open back window. The breaks in the panel afford views into the store behind while they also show the rear view of the garments being featured.

Marshall Field's has framed their mirrors with ornate, gilded frames to give a multi-view of gifts for the bride. In one display a mannequin has been imaginatively dressed up in gift ideas and the floor-placed mirrors give the viewer's a real eye-level look at the products.

Mirror mosaic tiles cover the spheres and turn them into "witches' balls" or the sparkling, light splattering icons of the 1950s and '60s. In Tiffany's windows it is a celebration of gift ideas along with the mirrored balls. The reflected spots of light provide the attraction that lures the viewer's eye towards the Tiffany products being featured up front.

THE LIMITED, Water Tower, Chicago, IL

MARSHALL FIELD'S, Water Tower, Chicago, IL

MARSHALL FIELD'S, Water Tower, Chicago, IL

TIFFANY & CO., Michigan Ave., Chicago, IL

ANN TAYLOR, Madison Ave., New York, NY

Large, small, rectangular, square, oval, gilded, gessoed, wood or plastic—frames are all of the above and much, much more. They can surround a painting, a mirror, a prized object—or left unfilled and used to focus on something it surrounds in space. They are focal points for focal points.

We have collected some interesting and diverse examples of where frames were used as decorative props. In Ann Taylor's window, the frames are painted off-white and filled in with panels covered with gray moiré fabric. With the addition of a cantilevered shelf, the frame becomes a displayer for the bags and accessories that go with the featured garments up front while those that are "unfilled" become non-obtrusive elements on the rear wall that carry out the theme and palette of the merchandise.

MAGASCHONI, Soho, New York, NY

SAKS FIFTH AVENUE, New York, NY

BERGDORF GOODMAN, Fifth Ave., New York, NY

In the very narrow, partially open-back window at Magaschoni, frames are suspended on gold ropes throughout the limited space. They do not center on or point up anything in particular but they do create a fun yet upscale setting for the garments on the mannequin. The pseudo trompe l'oeil artwork on the partial panel in the back carried through the frame theme.

Behind the stylized mannequin in the Saks Fifth Avenue window, the actual boiserie or woodwork of the architectural rear wall has been treated with gold and silver leaf turning the woodwork into "empty frames." Though they are "empty"—they do create a strong geometric pattern behind the flowery print dress up front and sort of "frame" the figure.

Bergdorf is making a "costume" statement with cascading framed fashion/costume drawings tumbling off the rear wall. On the front glass, there is an explanation for the original watercolor artwork and the Oscar de la Renta gown in the foreground.

WRAPPED

JEAN PAUL GAULTIER, Paris, France

Muslin is inexpensive and natural, it comes in wide widths and long lengths and is reusable. It is very versatile. In the hands of a clever display person it can do many things and create a sense of mystery as well.

Jean Paul Gaultier's window has the off-white fabric used to wrap things up. The unknown object on the left is now a riser for the handbag, while the rear panel is not only covered with muslin—but the black dress is "tied down" with ropes. Why? What does it mean? Does it really matter? It stopped you—made you look and ask questions—and you did get to see the offerings.

Saks Fifth Avenue is also wrapping things up including some chairs that are now floating overhead. Coarse heavy roping is used to tie it all together and set the stage for the white-on-white promotion. It could be resort wear. It could be a mystery? But—it "gotcha!!"

SAKS FIFTH AVENUE, New York, NY

BERGDORF GOODMAN, Fifth Ave., New York, NY

TARA JARMON, Stockholm, Sweden

The fabric falls free—it cascades like a waterfall down Bergdorf's overly tall window and caught in the flow are some white garments that are barely discernable in the white-on-white setting. However, the colored clothes on the headless mannequins more than survive the downward flow of fabric.

In Stockholm, the simple presentation is greatly enhanced by the textured rectangle behind the dress form. A piece of coarse muslin has been sprayed with bronze paint and then "crumpled" by hand and allowed to dry in that crinkly condition. Suspended from overhead in front of the crisp, white panel, the textured fabric adds interest, color and contrast to the merchandise.

MARSHHALL FIELD'S, State St., Chicago, IL

DKNY, Madison Ave., New York, NY

Masking is just another way of "framing" a display. There are many ways an object can be framed but what masking does—and usually to the display windpw itself—is cut down the viewer's field of vision and focus in on what is being featured. Shown on these pages are a variety of masking techniques.

Marshall Field actually cuts down the size of the window—actually cuts it in half and thus brings all of the viewer's attention to the illuminated and visible lower half of the window. The upper, blacked-out part, becomes an effective signboard for the promotion going on below.

DKNY's mask also serves to set the theme or look. The stenciled frame around the window focuses the viewer towards the clear, open central space where the three headless forms can be seen. Meanwhile, the "frame" is something like an old Valentine card or a lace doily and suggests an "old fashioned loveliness" that complements the fashions.

ANTHROPOLOGIE,
Soho, New York, NY

FROEHLICH FURS, Munich, Germany.
DESIGN: **Peter Rank, Deko Rank**

Froehlich Furs window, in Munich, is masked with sheets of foamcore and it highlights the cut out rectangular opening in which the fur clad mannequin is recessed. The striped violet and silver mask contrasts with the sharp yellow alcove and the yellow "popcorn" that gushes out to meet the front window.

Both Anthropologie and ABC Carpet & Home have used the same masking technique of painted artwork on the front glass. ABC Carpet, on lower Broadway, has painted a voluptuous, pull-back drape that cuts off part of the window's viewing area, and has completed the "drapery" on the back wall. Anthropologie has all but drowned its dress form in an ocean of waves and verse. Though the black outfit looms up behind the water-logged artwork, the viewer is drawn to come closer to read the lines of copy that ride the waves.

ABC CARPET & HOME, Broadway, New York, NY

One of a kind! Unique! More than special! When the retailer shows only one garment on a single mannequin in a window—all by itself—in the spotlight—it means this garment is truly one-of-a-kind—even if there are a dozen more in stock.

To show a "Solo" performer requires a setting and lighting that really makes the "star" appear brighter, more shimmering and alluring. The display team at Saks Fifth Avenue in New York City specializes in that one-of-a-kind window presentation as they show off top designer name fashions in their highly visible and auspicious windows.

Shown here are some recent examples of how Saks showed off their truly special garments. In one display the abstract mannequin in the caramel colored leather jacket is in a "spotlight"—with the circles behind it creating a focal frame for the figure. In another, the black and white clad abstract is centered for the viewer by the strings of twine that, in effect, frame it. The curving frames for the abstract in brown and black envelop the form and again gently bring the viewer's eye back to the outfit center stage.

When Saks uses their realistic mannequins—often to show off designer gowns—subtle, sophisticated room vignette settings are created. The display team brings in choice pieces: elegant and/or antique props, fine pieces of furniture, a chandelier, a potted palm tree—elements that suggest an ambiance in which that lovely mannequin in that elegant outfit would play a leading role.

SAKS FIFTH AVENUE, New York, NY

BERGDORF GOODMAN & BERGORF'S MEN'S STORE,
Fifth Ave., New York, NY

When your windows go up! up! up! and reach great heights, it is likely that your displays will soar as well. The talented and creative design team at Bergdorf Goodman, under the leadership of Linda Fargo and David Hoey, take full advantage of their extraordinarily tall windows. Rather than mask them down for focused, every-day-scale viewing, they make the height work for them by creating and installing these super, super, over-life-size, giant objects such as the birds, shown here, that swoop and perch in the all-white ambiance of these designed fashion windows.

Across the street in the more "traditional" display windows at The Men's Store, the designers created shopper-stoppers by overstating such everyday things as an architectural lamp, a tennis racket and a pipe. They not only get the shoppers' attention but brought them closer to see some of the Father's Day gifts that were being featured. The giant "avalanche" of falling boulders did the same thing while adding texture and suggesting the out-of-doors. Pebbles would not have been as effective or as much of a draw.

BERGDORF GOODMAN & BERGORF'S MEN'S STORE,
Fifth Ave., New York, NY

CHANEL, Fifth Ave., New York, NY

ST. JOHN, Fifth Ave., New York, NY

Really BIG TIME! A smaller "C" could have identified the Chanel name but the greatly overstated "C," shown here, not only serves as a big come-on, it provides a fabulous focal spot for the seated mannequin. She is encompassed and involved and dead-center in the almost circular "bull's eye"—the center of the window.

Ring-a-ding-ding and add a few more rings! If it weren't for the oversized metal rings hanging in the St. John window, the viewer might not have gotten the fashion message being relayed. The connected dangling rings replay—in a big way—the rings around the waist of the mannequin on the right.

BLOOMINGDALE'S, Lexington Ave., New York, NY

Scaling up is also BIG TIME at Bloomingdale's where the over-developed props play against the mannequins and come out the winning attractions. The unlikeliness of the size—when compared with what is "normal"—turns these giant props into attention grabbers.

BLOOMINGDALE'S,
Lexington Ave., New York, NY

HARVEY NICHOLS, London, UK
VISUAL MERCHANDISING CONTROLLER: **Janet Wardley**
WINDOW DISPLAY MANAGER: **Laura O'Connor**
PHOTOGRAPHY: **in-house**

Harvey Nichols also plays fast and furious—and colorfully—and amusingly—with scale when it comes to adding pizzazz to high fashion windows. The store's design team, working under Janet Wardley and Laura O'Connor, presented this tasty, if voluminous, snack in the Harvey Nichols windows in Knightsbridge in London. Milk splashes out of a giant carton while pink icing oozes out between the layers of a humongous cake. The pink and blue icing/splash become the featured colors in the clothing on view.

For the HN Manchester store, the team came up with a Beauty & The Beast theme even if the "beast" is only an overgrown teddy bear. In keeping with the "blow up"—some of the letters that appear in the newspapers that cover the walls and floor are shown in an exaggerated scale that ties in with teddy.

At Shreve Crump & Low in Boston, Lucy-Ann Bouwman, the visual display director, used full size children's bicycles to give—in her words—"a superb contradiction to the opening of the window, and deliver the humor/whimsy of what can be placed in a typical area of a jewelry window display." Here it is the scaled down version of the bicycle that is still oversized in relation to the small precious pieces of jewelry shown with it.

HARVEY NICHOLS, Manchester, UK

SHREVE CRUMP & LOW, Boston, MA
VISUAL DISPLAY DIRECTOR: **Lucy-Ann Bouwman**
PHOTOGRAPHY: **Chris Akelian**

BARNEYS NEW YORK, Madison Ave., New York, NY
CREATIVE DIRECTOR: **Simon Doonan**

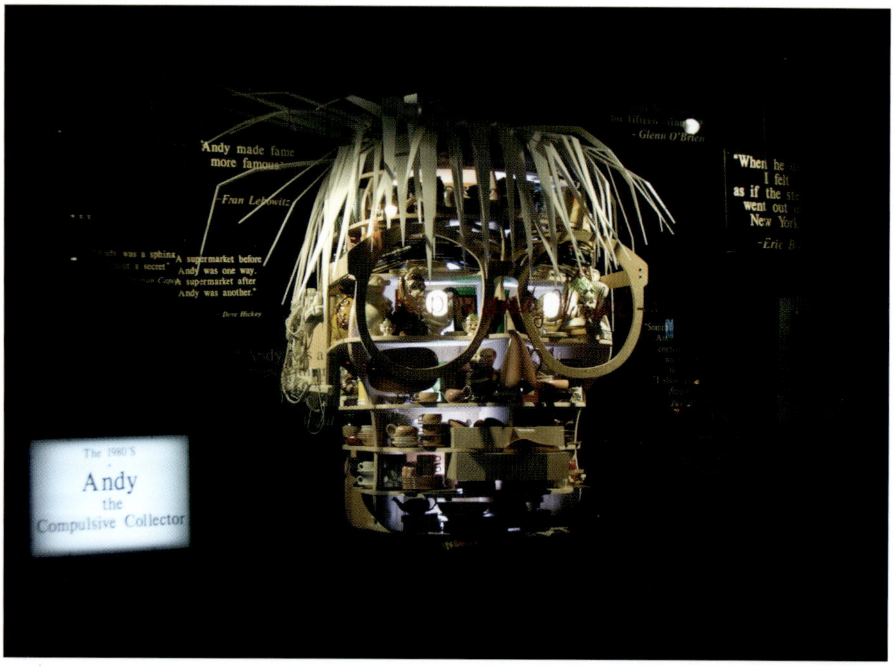

"This is my 20th anniversary of designing the holiday windows at Barneys, and I wanted to do something totally over the top," said Simon Doonan, the Creative Director for the Barneys New York stores that stretch across the U.S. from Madison Avenue in New York City to Seattle, Washington. What could be more "over the top" or a "topper shopper stopper" than a salute to Andy Warhol?

The main windows, on Madison Avenue, focused on the different stages in Warhol's life: Andy the Illustrator, Andy the Compulsive Collector, Andy the Factory Boy, and Andy the Social Butterfly. The final window in the series featured portraits of Warhol created by children from the East Harlem School, and these one-of-a-kind artworks were sold off to benefit the school. Across the country, each Barneys store had a similar "charity" window that benefited a local institution.

"Andy was an important, serious artist, but he also had a frivolous side. He loved

shopping. He was proud of his commercial illustrations and his store window designs. I always think of him as a kind of patron saint of American retail," added Doonan.

To further promote the Andy Warhol theme, a special shopping bag was designed as well as a gift pack of Campbell's soup cans. In the store there were limited editions of Warhol gift cards, Warhol/Levis clothes decorated with Warhol iconography and a special holiday catalog "peppered with his philosophical musings."

Senior Window Director David Hoey and his team of artists and craftspeople created a fantasy of props and scenes that filled the 35 windows of Bergdorf Goodman that stretched across Fifth Avenue and extended part way down East 57th and 58th streets. The five main windows that depicted The Art of Celebrating showed off the many ways different people can enjoy the pleasures of the holiday season. The suggested ways were: Entertain, Decorate, Cultivate, Recollect and Astound.

And—astound they did! Once again the viewers were treated to a feast of fabulous filled-to-overflowing panoramas with unusual settings, unbelievable animals, and odd and breathtaking props. In the Decorate window "two mannequins have gone wild by using thousands of gingerbread cookies, cakes and desserts." Each piece was made in-house, iced and decorated by the design staff who worked almost 24/7 to affect these one-of-a-kind windows. "The result is a gingerbread obsession: brown and white fills every inch of the window—delicious and delicate, with lace details—a feast for the eyes smothered in icing and the holiday spirit."

That same delight in detail made each window in the series a thoroughly eye-filling visual experience.

BERGDORF GOODMAN, New York, NY
SENIOR WINDOW DIRECTOR: **David Hoey**

It was a trip around the world for the viewers of the holiday windows at Bloomingdale's as each of the main windows depicted gift-givers from many lands giving gifts. Viewers were able to meet Father Frost of Russia, La Befana of Italy, Sister Klaas of The Netherlands, St. Basil of Greece and, of course, our own American-styled Santa Claus. The gift-givers were not only international but of both genders. In addition it was ecumenical in that the gift-giving extended to Chanukah and Kwanzaa as well. Each setting featured a revolving gift-giver in a glistening snow globe—or a family gathered around—exuding warmth and tradition. Each of the figures was set against either an architectural background or a natural environment that was typical of the land from which they came. To reinforce the idea that this was a World Celebration, each window was framed in a silver-beaded proscenium with longitude and latitude lines layered in relief. "Bloomingdale's windows were a tribute to a magical time of the year when all cultures celebrate—whether it is Christmas, Chanukah, Kwanzaa, New Years—or even a magical snowfall."

As many other stores did this year, Bloomingdale's tied in with "giving" as well as "getting." Chris Botti, the celebrated jazz trumpeter, was saluted and his newest CD, *December,* was sold in the store and the proceeds of the sale of the CDs were donated to AmeriCare: a humanitarian disaster relief organization. Chris Botti was featured in a live performance that was followed by the opening of these windows.

BLOOMINGDALE'S, New York, NY

LORD & TAYLOR, New York, NY
DESIGNED BY: **Manoel Renha,** Div. VP, Creative Director for 5th Avenue Windows and **The L&T Design Team**

This year's Lord & Taylor windows did not fly off to Never-Never-Land or the Land of Make Believe—or the place where fairy tales are set. They didn't go round the world either. Lord & Taylor celebrated "It's A Gift of Joy" and showcased that JOY with three dimensional "pictures" or "postcards" from a magical family scrapbook that showed different periods of American Christmas celebrations.

Personal comments and mementos were used to develop the "stories" and each illustration was encased in an exquisite frame of that period. As a giant Victorian fan opened and closed, young lovers kissed for the first time in 1843. This was "Joy." Victorian carolers, a family gathered to play music and a Christmas tree revolving atop a music box set the scene for "Harmony" in 1861. "Peace" came in 1897 with the famed Dakota building on the skyline and children building a snowman. The kitchen setting of 1905 showed "Family Unity" as preparations were going on and in the grand dining room with Tiffany glass windows—the family was toasting to health and happiness. It was like a scene out of *The Night Before Christmas*—"Hope" and the year was 1925, while grandma, in 1954, looked at her scrapbook and reminisced with the children.

"Whimsical large mechanicals have been introduced to our usual mix of superbly executed animated figures. Each of the Fifth Avenue windows revealed memories of happy past holiday seasons and all the wonderful things that mean Christmas. Charming scenes of elaborate historical detail convey the universal emotions that symbolize the spirit of the season: Love, Harmony, Peace, Family Unity, Hope and Joy."

Lord & Taylor, in the spirit of the season, presented donations to Feed the Children and to Cassidy's Place, a therapeutic facility for disadvantaged local children. It was named for Kathie Lee Gifford's daughter. Ms. Gifford and Larry Jones were joined by the Young People's Chorus of New York City to perform at the opening ceremonies for these holiday windows.

Christmas
Greetings
May Christmas
Its magic spell
Make all things
All things well

Fifty years go by so quickly when you LOVE each other
My first kiss with William... it feels like only yesterday. That wonderful party at the Benson's... under the mistletoe...

North Pole
It was the night before Christmas and the children were JOYOUS, sure that they had seen Santa out the window. It took some time to get them to bed so we were a bit late leaving for our party!

POST CARD

MACY'S, Herald Square, New York, NY
DIRECTOR OF WINDOWS: **Paul Olszewski**
ASST. WINDOW DIRECTOR: **Douglas Fowler**
PRODUCED BY: **Spaeth Design,** New York, NY
AUDIO ENGINEER: **Manu Sawkar,** New York, NY
LIGHTING: **Joshua Epstein,** New York, NY

Paul Olszewski, Macy's Herald Square's Director of Windows, provided New Yorkers and their guests with passports to a trip through six fantasy lands where they could experience "Trees of the World." In each stunning presentation, the windows literally came "out of the box." The window environment extended onto the exterior of the building—framing and enveloping the scene and "viewers became part of the experience through highly interactive elements."

The "lands" that were visited included Peace, Harmony, Joy, Beauty, Friendship and Love. Each "tree" was shown from a unique perspective: from underneath—"to the view from inside the trunk of the tree; from the vantage point above a spinning tree decorated by fairies—to an underwater Christmas festival presided over by a mermaid and a giant octopus." The voyage of the imagination ended when the two travelers—inside the windows—were helped by a fire-breathing dragon in a forest of Christmas trees to blow beautiful glass ornaments that end up in a tree house. Here our travelers helped Santa with his preparations for Christmas.

The travelers—outside the windows—got to help the two inside. Much of the action in the windows was controlled by touch-pads on the exterior surface of the windows where viewers could "initiate a sequence of animation, lighting, music and sound all synchronized to work with the six new arrangements of the classic carol *Oh Christmas Tree*." For an extra spin on fantasy/reality, the dragon's eyes were actually video monitors that showed the crowds outside working the action inside the windows.

The success of the high-tech snowflake light show that was introduced on the façade of Saks Fifth Avenue two years ago, once again made snowflakes the central theme for the holiday décor of the store. A new holiday spectacle—an LED light show choreographed to a modern version of Carol of the Bells—was introduced this year and the windows featured a fabulous, glittering and glistening set of frosty scenes.

Thousands of Swarovski crystals were used to fabricate the shimmering and sparkling props and figures that told the story of ice crystals that dreamt of becoming part of the perfect snowflake. In a succession of window tableaux, viewers were invited to follow Allie, Tay-Tay, Chip, Winnie and Timmy—five "rag-tag ice crystals"—as they searched to join a snowflake. They are led by the North Wind on this journey to the discovery that each one of us is beautiful and unique and all that we have to do is realize that for ourselves. "Surrounded by a glittery art deco landscape, each snowflake they discovered on their way was more fantastical than the last, from giant kaleidoscopic flakes to a fantastical reinvention of Busby Berkley."

As part of the snowflake holiday trim, there was a performance on November 20th (when the windows were opened) by students of the American Ballet Theater dancing to the Land of the Snow from The Nutcracker ballet. The performance was tied in with a special charity drive and the appearance of Marla Thomas for the St. Jude Children's Research Hospital. The noted designer, Valentino, flew in to appear in support of this charity event. Throughout the holiday shopping season shoppers had the opportunity to join Saks in making a donation to St. Jude—as part of their purchases. Steve Sadove, CEO Saks Fifth Avenue, said, "We are thrilled to partner with St. Jude Children's Research Hospital on the 'Thanks & Giving' program. It's a groundbreaking initiative and a great way to share the generous spirit of the season."

HENRI BENDEL, Fifth Ave., New York, NY

MACY'S, 34th St., New York, NY

Snowflakes—giant electrified ones—covered Saks Fifth Avenue's façade and snow and snowflakes "fell" in their windows which were shown in our June issue. Here is more of the snowstorm that hit New York for Christmas.

Giant filigree neon snowflakes floated in Henri Bendel's open back window. The crisp, cool buzz of the neon added a real chill to this display of mostly red merchandise.

Foamcore snowflakes heavily dusted with diamond dust and sparklers filled the toiletries windows at Macy's where the gift cosmetics and perfumes were amusingly tied into the kaleidoscopic design of the window, almost as though it were a Busby Berkley production.

DIOR, Madison Ave., New York, NY

A single, dynamic burst of stars took over the right side of Dior's mirror backed window. The silvery stars were all heading towards the single midnight blue gown highlighted in the otherwise deep blue environment.

Stars fell by the dozens in Escada's blacked out window where the realistic mannequins in their bright red festive gowns were literally and figuratively reaching for the stars—and making it!

ESCADA, E. 57th St., New York, NY

Even Christmas is not "same old—same old" at HN. Each year the un-traditional becomes part of the store brand's tradition. In almost circus-like settings made up of hundreds of small and mostly recycled and reused materials, and with each window flushed in bright colors ranging from "traditional" red and green to "untraditional" orange, violet and turquoise, especially made-up mannequins by Bodyline again feature the almost white skin tone that seems to be an HN signature look. Here they are complemented by dark wigs as they show off the newest fashions. Like one of Simon Doonan's "clutter" windows at Barneys, the hundreds of small, individual elements come together masterfully to create these eye-popping and attention getting displays.

Our thanks to Janet Wardley and Laura O'Connor for sharing these projects with our readers and for helping us to explain how HN keeps their brand ever new, ever evolving and ever involving.

HARVEY NICHOLS, London, UK
VISUAL MERCHANDISING CONTROLLER: **Janet Wardley**
WINDOW DISPLAY MANAGER: **Laura O'Connor**
PROPS: **Icon Studio** and **Artefacts**
PHOTOGRAPHY: **Melvyn Vincent**

The design team, working under the directorship of Victor Johnson, Senior Manager of Presentation for the Ann Taylor chain, intended their Holiday trim to be—"A glimpse into Ann's home at holiday time where our featured collections could be surrounded by keepsakes, heirlooms and decorative touches that reflect the spirit and celebration of the season. A home setting provided us with two opportunities: the white and silver trim creates an elegant backdrop for occasion apparel, while furniture pieces provide venues for showcasing gift items such as accessories, jewelry, candles and frames as the season progresses."

A suggestion of depth was created in each installation by the framing of the windows with a proscenium of drapery. Victor Johnson explains, "The overall composition in each location is intended to be dramatic in scale, so as to attract the attention of pedestrian traffic, but ultimately intimate details in each window help to pull the viewer in." Velvet drapery, satin fringe, antiqued mirrors, mercury glass finials, polished metal candlesticks, silver leafed garland, monogrammed linens, silver leafed furniture such as dressing tables, chairs, etc, "instill a sense of sparkle, sophistication and detail in the windows." Typical is the dressing table with delicate glass finials, perfume bottles, necklaces and bracelets, etched mirrors, framed pictures and a bengaline runner monogrammed with a cursive "A.T."—for Ann Taylor—embroidered on it.

For the flagship New York store on 60th Street and Madison Avenue, awnings of white and silver garland were constructed over the windows to give them more prominence. They were encrusted with lights "to heighten the drama and luster of the installation."

Shown here are some of the Ann Taylor stores in New York City as they were festively decorated for the holidays.

ANN TAYLOR, New York, NY
SR. MANAGER OF PRESENTATION: **Victor Johnson**
PHOTOS: **Courtesy of Ann Taylor**

HOME FOR THE HOLIDAYS @ ANN TAYLOR

ANN TAYLOR, New York, NY
SR. MANAGER OF PRESENTATION:
Victor Johnson
PHOTOS: **Courtesy of Ann Taylor**

ANN TAYLOR

ANN TAYLOR

ANN TAYLOR

The inspiration for this lovely installation in the Hermès of Paris boutique in Boston was a book, "Ma Bonne Etoile" (My Lucky Star), and Hermès' perfume Eau des Merveilles. For these windows, Lucy Ann Bouwman, the designer, took viewers—like the lovers in the book—on a magical journey to Paris and like the book's pair—"to see the monuments of Paris illuminated against the night sky—and fill them with excitement and anticipation of what the evening holds."

Two champagne glasses and the lovers outlined in lights and a display of gifts for "him" tie in with the Eiffel Tower, while twinkling light constellations, the winged foot of Nike and music notes that suggest the sound of marching bands marching around the Arc de Triomphe are used to present Hermès bags, gloves and shoes.

With the outline of a face "blowing stars like good night kisses," the window that features the dome of Sacre Coeur church on Montmartre was combined with children's "warm" gift suggestions. Women's wear, sparkling shoes and Hermes fine china pay homage to the trend setting French Woman and Notre Dame Cathedral.

Lucy Ann Bouwman explains, "We built the architectural structures and covered them with royal blue angel suede, then embedded them with blue and white twinkle lights. The clouds were fashioned from copper wire and covered with gold and silver leaf." She adds, "Holiday window displays are important to retail because they are not only a glimpse into the heart of the store, but allow visual people to express themselves more fully than at other times of the year. They enable designers to hold nothing back in creating a memorable experience that stirs something inside the passerby, and contribute to the overall magic of the season by being a true gift to the consumer."

Thank you, Lucy Ann!

HERMÈS OF PARIS, Boston, MA
DESIGN: **Lucy Ann Bouwman**

HENRI BENDEL, Fifth Ave. New York, NY

If any color says "Christmas"—it must be *red.* Red hot—real rich, warm and friendly—red is a color that glows with tradition.

Bendel's open back window was bursting out with vibrant red—from the all red figure on the left to the floating, shimmering, sparkling red tree on the right. Hanging from the tree were chandeliers and wire bird cages—in red—and dozens of red birds bedecked the branches of the tree. A proscenium of crinkly red material and a gold stenciled border on the glass framed the scene.

Lord & Taylor featured red evening gowns in their fashion windows which were beautifully and richly decorated room vignettes. The elegant gowns on the realistic mannequins were complemented by the chandeliers, draperies and period furniture that fleshed out the scenes.

Sony celebrated the season and showed off a wealth of giftable products in a flurry of red: red frames, red ribbon-wrapped boxes, red toys, red glitter and tinsel and a Christmas tree made up of gift boxes tied up and decorated in red. There were even red faced—and handed—mannequins dressed in—what else?—RED.

LORD & TAYLOR, Fifth Ave., New York, NY

SONY, Madison Ave., New York, NY

TIFFANY & CO., Fifth Ave., New York, NY

CALVIN KLEIN, Fifth Ave., New York, NY

ESCADA, E. 57th St., New York, NY

Cool blues, aquas and lots of white appeared to create a COOL Christmas palette.

It was all ice and snow in Tiffany's windows with icicle trimmed pine boughs, birch branches embedded in sparkly snow and ice skates to traverse the ice covered surfaces. The dramatic but chilly blue lighting added to the chill while accentuating the crystal clear quality of many of the crystal gifts presented in the windows.

Bare branches, snow and white doves set the holiday scene at Calvin Klein's boutique. A snow covered plane swept through the window with bare, snowy branches reaching up to separate the two dressed headless figures up front from the store visible beyond. Doves nested and rested in and around this icicle dripping setting.

Flickering aqua lights pierced the cold, deep blue sky behind the reclining figure in white gown and fur coat in the Escada window. Aqua and white frosted globes rested on the snow covered floor along with spider-web balls accented with aqua twinkle lights. The blue lights, hidden in the snow, gently illuminated the spheres or oversized "ornaments" while adding to the chilly look that said it's a Cool Christmas at Escada.

BROOKS BROS., Fifth Ave., New York, NY

STEUBEN GLASS, Fifth Ave., New York, NY

Christmas trees of all shapes, sizes, finishes and colors took over windows to get across the holiday message. Some were frankly fake and made no attempt at realism while others exuded the scent of pine forests and the great out-of-doors.

Brooks Bros. went for a traditional "Home for the Holidays" effect with a welcoming red door covered with a snow powdered wreath and draped in pine cone trimmed garlands. The evergreen trees sparkled with bee lights that played off the glistening snow. A rather unusual "tree of ties" arose from behind some of the green ones. It was really unique enough not to have had to compete with the realistic ones for attention—in the same window.

Aside from the frosted crystal tree centered in Steuben's window, the white, feathery trees carried forward the holiday essence as did the white tree in the Coach window. The shimmering life-sized white deer added a fairy tale look to the scene.

Swarovski's fanciful tree was wrought of wire and finished in white. Swarovski crystals and beads were used to trim the scroll-like tree and these were complemented by the red ornaments. The two dimensional tree was backed up by a sheet of cool blue plastic that added a feeling of iciness.

Down in Puerto Rico, Frank Caballero took a warmer attitude towards the holiday with tree a made up of silvery shoe horns assembled over a cone. These complemented the mannequins abbreviated costumes, also made of the shoe horns. The red floor and background were "traditional" and just right for this clime.

GALERIA, Plaza Las Americas, Puerto Rico
DESIGN: **Frank Caballero**
PHOTOGRAPHER: **Pascal Fontana**

SWAROVSKI, Madison Ave., New York, NY

COACH, Madison Ave., New York, NY

THE BAY, Queen St., Toronto, ON, Canada
DESIGN DIRECTOR: **Ana Fernandes**

Giving a little ends up with a lot of promotional value when The Bay in Toronto takes on Valentine's Day. With red hearts, lots of red in the lighting, the propping and the fashions being presented—and the numerous post-its surrounding the circular target—the "message" certainly does get across.

The message—written across the front glass—is "Helping to forgive and forget—give a little." If the viewer has any doubt of what "little" should be "given," The Bay has provided numerous visual clues from a closet full of Manolo Blahnk shoes to costume jewelry, toiletries, cosmetics and—of course—the new season's fashions.

THE BAY, Queen St., Toronto, ON, Canada
DESIGN DIRECTOR: **Ana Fernandes**